Vendel and Dark Age Desgn

AF621158

By Igor D. Górewicz
Illustrated by Marek Piłaszewicz
Translation by Karolina Socha-Duśko
Cover design by Igor D. Górewicz, Marek Piłaszewicz

Originially Published in Szczecin, 2013

Triglav Books is a trademark of „Trzygłów" – Pokazy Historyczne Igor D. Górewicz gorewicz@wp.pl
www.wydawnictwo.triglav.com.pl

Published under agreement by Winged Hussar Publishing, LLC,
1525 Hulse Rd, Unit 1
Point Pleasant, NJ 08742

ISBN 978-1-950423-48-4
LCN

Bibliographical References and Index
1. History 2. Slavic/Vendel 3. Designs

For more information on Pike and Powder Publishing Group, LLC,
visit us at www.whpsupplyroom.com & www.wingedhussarpublishing.com

twitter: @WingHusPubLLC
facebook: @WingedHussarPublishingLlc

INTRODUCTION

Years have passed since the publication of the first volume of Ornamental Design. The subsequent volumes devoted to the Slavs and Vikings in Polish, English and German languages have reached the thousands of modern warriors across the Old Continent. Many have crossed the oceans and are now serving the Vikings in the Americas and in Australia. Many viewers at Viking Age festivals have taken with them a copy of our catalogs as an inspiration for modern life coming from the depths of history—to embellish their lives and enrich them with a deeper symbolism. Working on, and viewing the Viking Age ornamentation one can clearly see that although very original, it was not created ex nihilo. Obviously, it is the result of an evolution. So where should we look for its predecessors? Where is the source? These are of course many, including the heritage of the Latin and Greek antiquity, which was reaching north via Ravenna and Aachen and the Byzantium—and the culture of the East: the Eurasian Steppe culture. The greatest source is early cultures of the European Barbaricum. These, in turn, are themselves very complex, as a result of multiple influences and processes. The Viking Era was preceded by the Dark Age, known in Scandinavia as the Vendel Time, in the British Isles as the Anglo-Saxon period. These are also the main foci of our interest in this volume. The aesthetic heritage that it left behind is striking in its beauty and yet steeped in the semantic content. The plaques (pressblecks) are adorning the Vendel or Anglo-Saxon warriors' helmets are miniature works of art, at the same time containing extremely complex mythological transfer. They express role models, tell stories of mental and physical transformation, and constitute an incentive to do great deeds, or a request for custody of the Gods. Each decoration from a drinking horn can be a masterpiece in itself, but only the entire composition is breathtaking in its beauty but its message. This is because by reading into its symbolism, we can see it as a story of brave warriors and their great chief; the dedication and loyalty to the grave, generosity, courage, duty, fellowship, mutual care and support.

Again, we took a closer look at buckles, metal elements, horns, swords, helmets, shields, brooches, pendants and we extracted ornaments placed on them. The selection of materials focused in particular on certain regions, including Scandinavia and England. The most extremely decorative and characteristic findings of Gotland's Vendel era are the most extensively presented ones. The collection of motifs copied from helmets and shields found in the graves of elite warriors at Vendel and Valsgärde is especially eye capturing. Among the English designs, attention is drawn to the diverse and rich collection coming from the famous royal burial at Sutton Hoo.
The catalog is closed with descriptions of the locations of each find, the most accurate dating, cultural context, and possible symbolic

meaning—where possible. The internal cross-references will help the reader get a glimpse of aesthetic the realities of the era, or deliberately select a particular ornament. The source of the original reproduction and/or the information acquired about each find are provided in square brackets as a row of figures where the first digit is the number corresponding to the list of literature references following the descriptions. Following the dot there is the second digit, indicating the number of the page in the source publication, or if the reference is an illustration, it is labeled as "Fig." or "Table." The commas separate subsequent page numbers or images within the same book, while the semicolon separates the positions which we refer to. If the source of an illustration is an image we have prepared, then give the name of the museum where the photograph was taken is provided. In one case we also provide a website address we took the image from.

Igor D. Górewicz
Szczecin, October 24, 2013

CATALOGUE

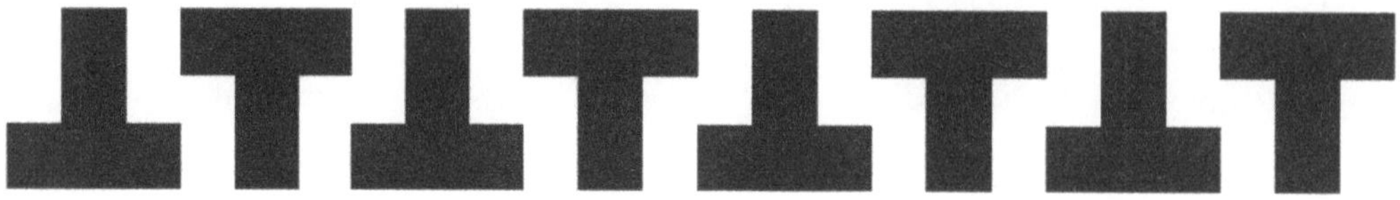

001 – Deep engraved motif made up from T-shaped elements. Smiss, Gotland, ca. 700-750 CE [11.Table 239, Fig. 1965; 10.69, Fig. 1965]

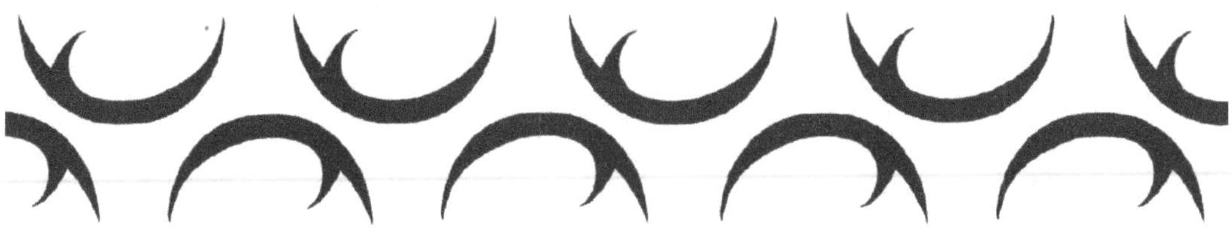

002 – Lunular ornament on the guard of a Frankish Mannheim type sword, Storra, Gotland, ca. 750-800 CE [11.Table 298, Fig. 2345; 10.83, Fig. 2345]

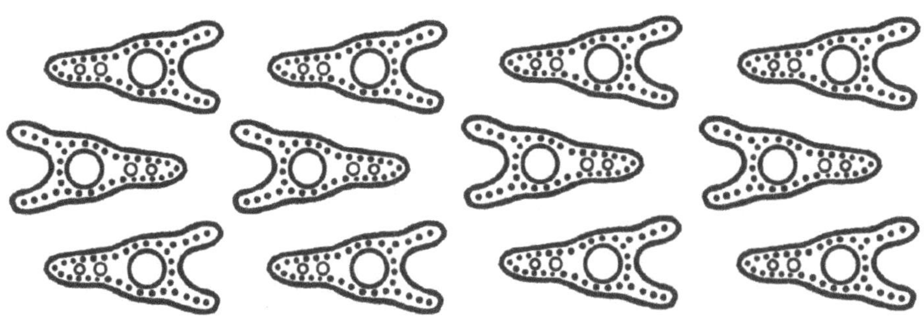

003 – Ornament on the hoop of a bronze belt buckle, Gotland, ca. 550-600 CE, (Also see 157) [11.Table 25, Fig. 269; 10.20, Fig. 269]

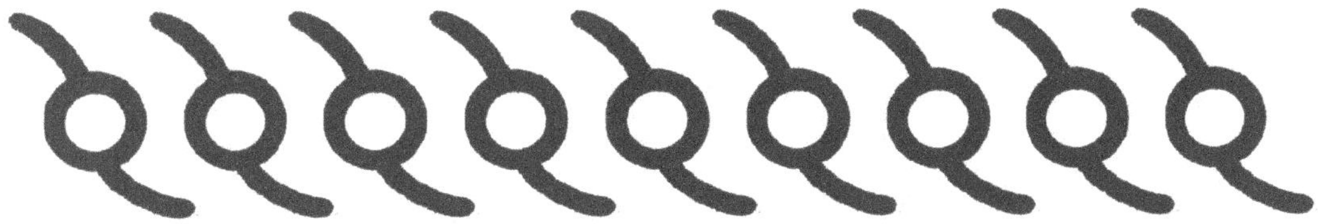

004 – Niello technique ornament from silver plaques on the throat of a scabbard, Nydam Bog, Nydam II find, ca. 400 CE [15.417-418]

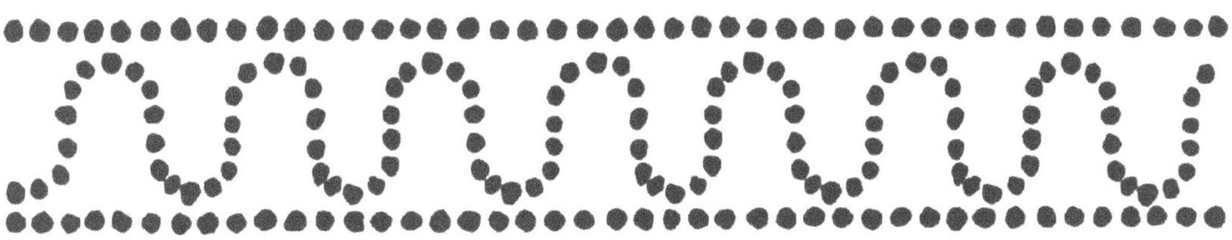

005 – Geometric pattern from a round bronze attachment of a sword and scabbard, Roes, Gotland, ca. 550-600 CE [11.Table 55, Fig. 535; 10.28, Fig. 535]

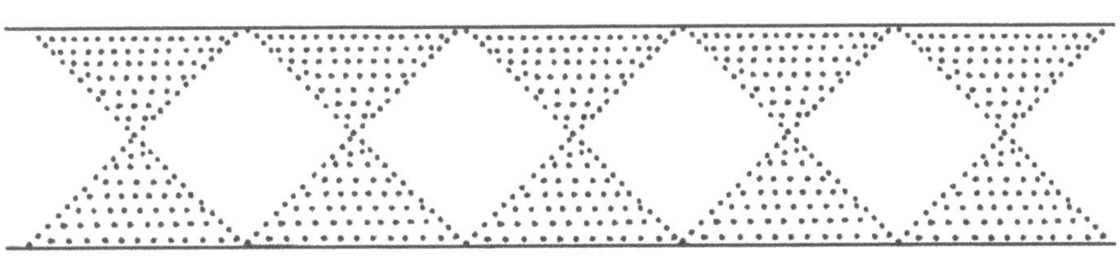

006 – Triangular motif, sinked on gilded bronze plates on the reinforcing bars of a Spangenhelm type helmet from Stössen, 1. Mid-6th c. [3.176, dwg. 99]

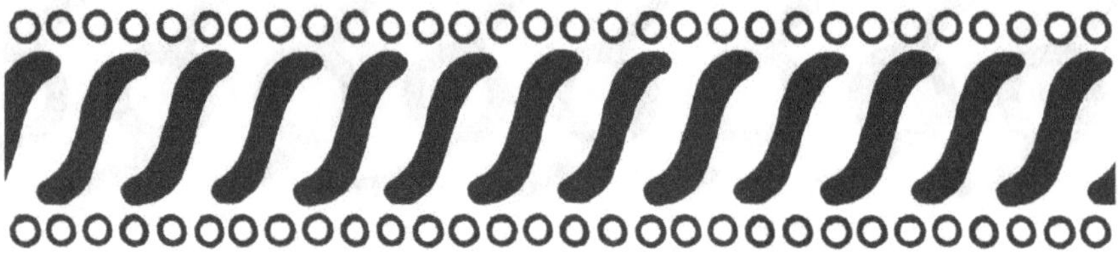

007 – Ornament from a round, bronze belt attachment, Gotland, ca. 550-600 CE [11. Table 35, Fig. 379; 10.23, Fig. 379]

008 – Motif repeated on what was probably the boss of a shield, Bjärs, Gotland, ca. 700-750 CE [11.Table 258, Fig. 2088; 10.74, Fig. 2088]

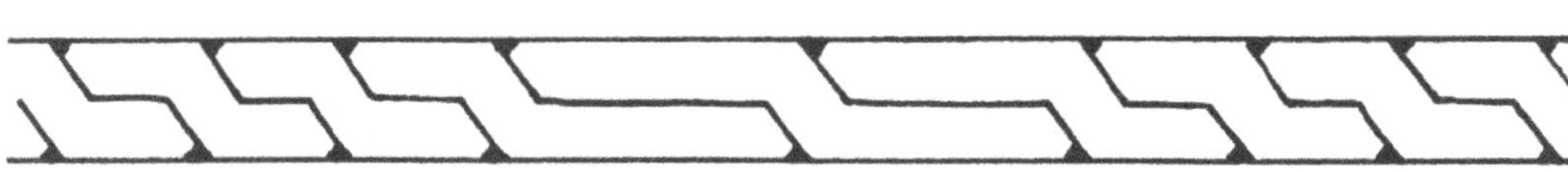

009 – A plaid ornament on the lower and upper bone guard of a sword, Bjärs, Gotland, ca. 600-650 CE [11.Table 132, Fig. 1179; 10.45, Fig. 1179]

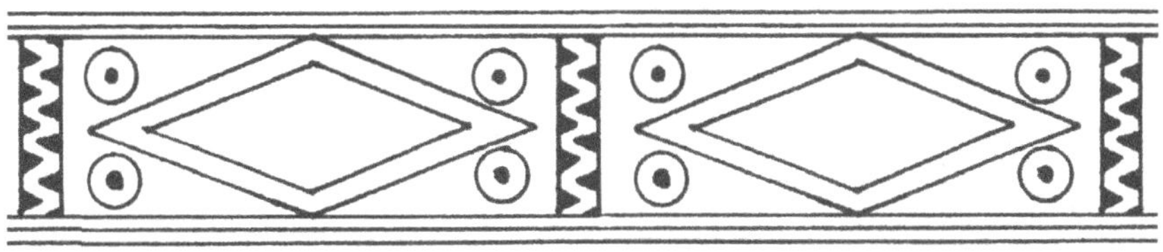

010 – Carved ornaments on an antler comb. Such ornaments survived at least until the Viking Age, Storra, Gotland, ca. 700-750 CE [11.Table 242, Fig. 1997; 10.70, Fig. 1997]

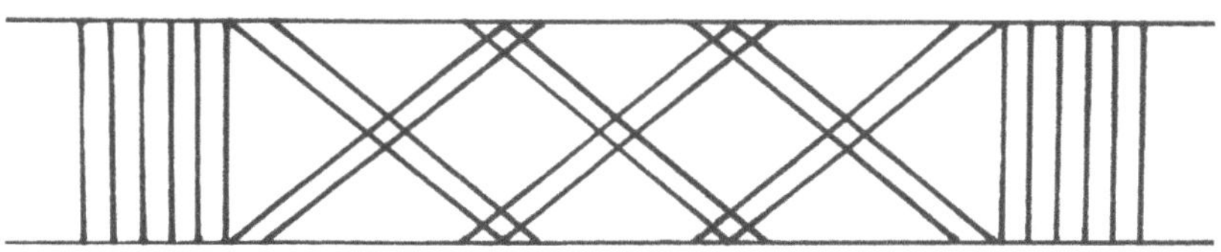

011 – Ornament on a door key. Gotland, ca. 550-600 CE, [11.Table. 44, Fig. 454; 10.25, Fig. 454]

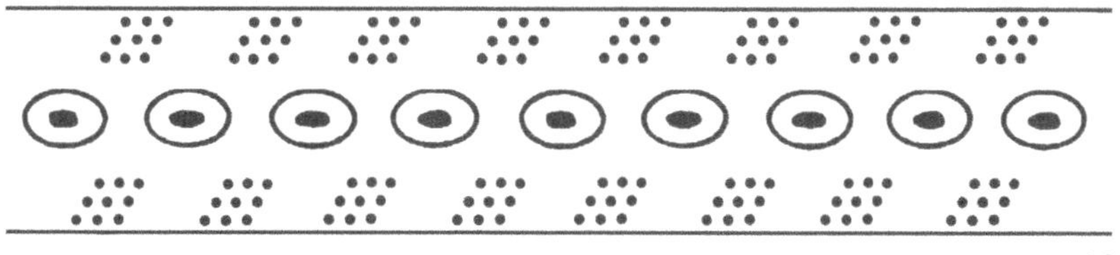

012 – Pattern on a buckle hoop (See variant in 015) Gotland, ca. 550-600 CE, [11.Table 18, Fig. 183; 10.17, Fig. 183]

013 – Ornament on belt attachment. Lombardic import (Italy), Roes, Gotland, ca. 550-600 CE [11.Table 31, Fig. 349; 10.22, Fig. 349]

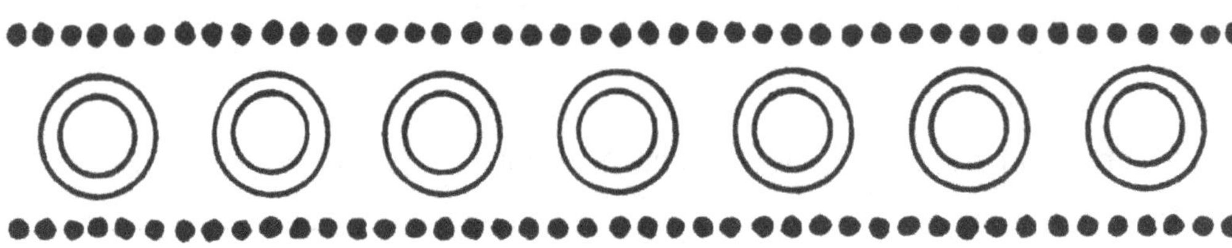

014 – Geometric element of a round bronze element of a sword and scabbard set. Roes, Gotland, ca. 550-600 CE [11.Table 55, Fig. 536; 10.28, Fig. 536]

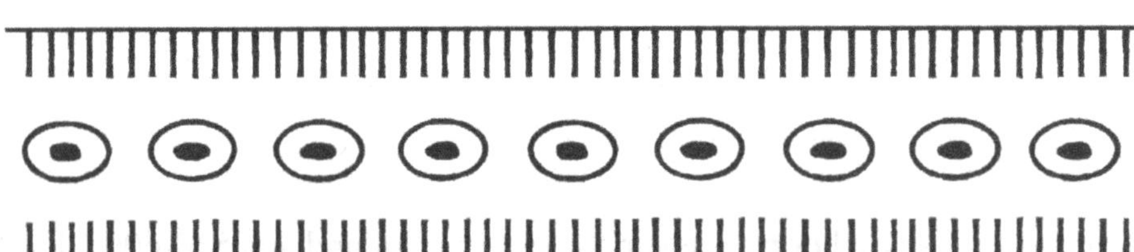

015 – See 012

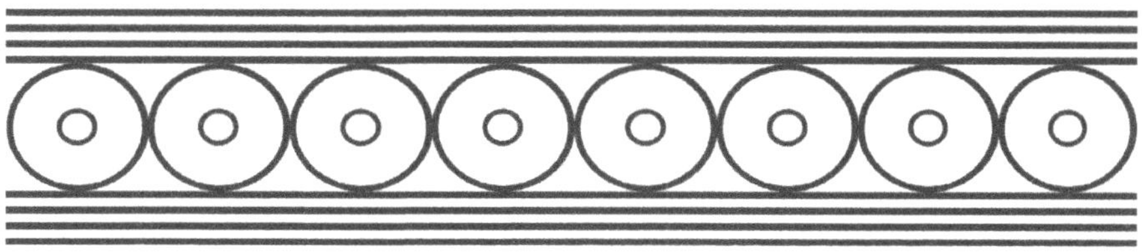

016 – Ornament on a plate surrounding the mouth of the face plate of the Sutton Hoo helmet (See 047) [4.46-49, Plate III]

017 – Ornament on the neck of a shield boss, Barshaldershed, Gotland ca. 550-600 CE [11.Table 70, Fig. 627; 10.30, Fig. 627]

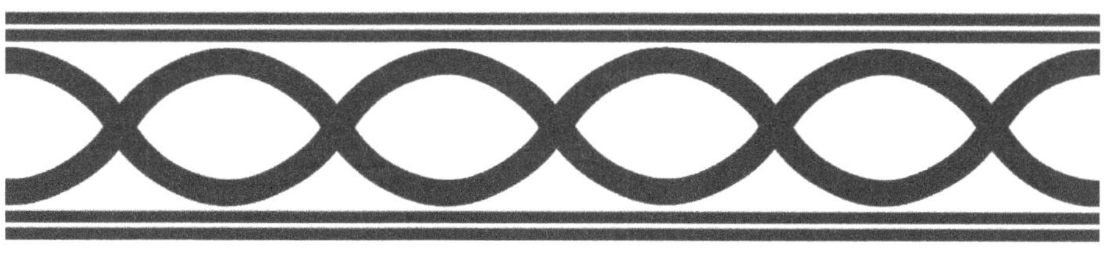

018 – Thick red color ornament on a shield discovered next to the pine boat in Nydam Bog, deposition horizon Nydam Ib, early 4th c. [6.263,268-269, Fig.10]

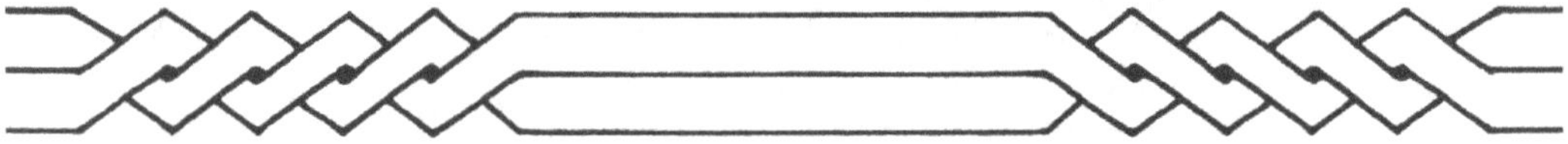

019 – Ornament on the rim of a round fibula. Roes, Gotland, ca. 650-700 CE [11.Table 168, Fig. 1396; 10.52-53, Fig. 1396]

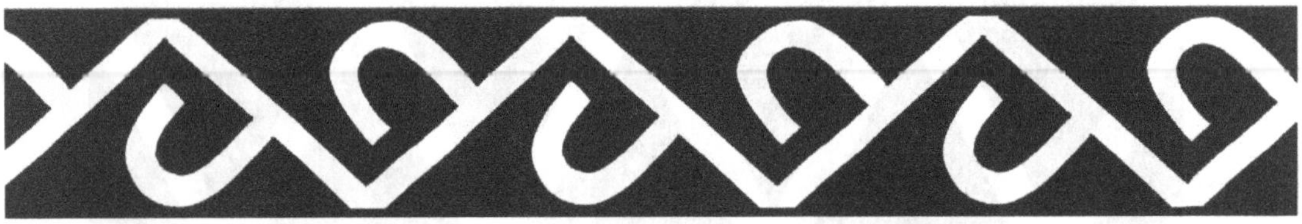

020 – Ornamentation found around the curved picture stone from Sanda church on Gotland. For other motifs from the same stone see 187, 244, and 245 [15.303-304, Fig.11]

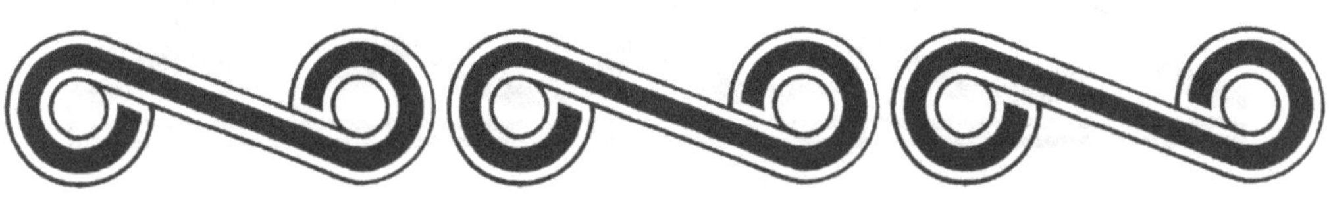

021 – Patten on the hoop of a Ostrogoth belt buckle. Romagna (Italy), 6th c. (Also see 261) [12.61, Fig. 16]

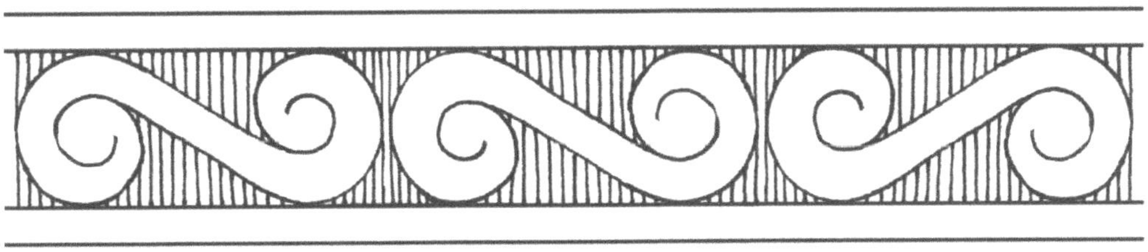

022 – Niello inlaid spiral ornamentation on a sword's bronze pommel from the Nydam Bog, deposition horizon Nydam IV, ca. 450-475 CE [6.281-282, Fig. 34]

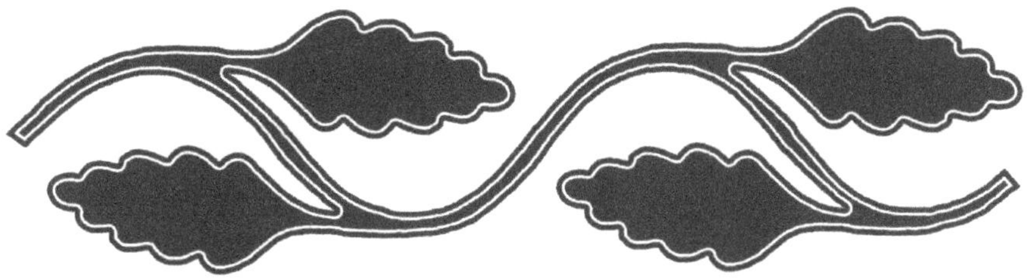

023 – Tendril pattern from a gilded box from a female burial in the Köln Damengrab). Probable burial of a Merovingian dynasty member, ca. 530/540 CE [5.41-42]

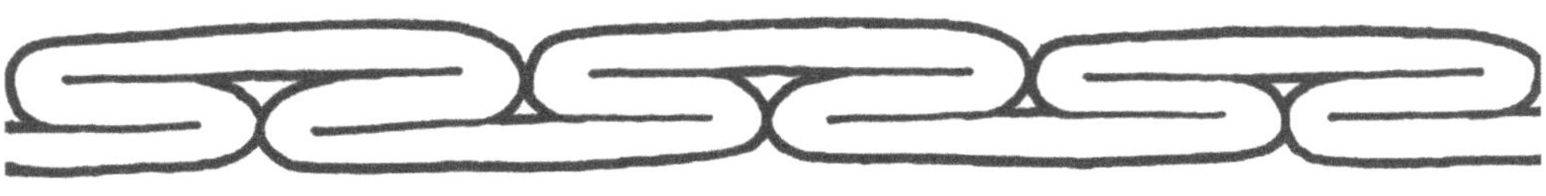

024 – One of the ornaments on the Hornhausen stela (Germany), depicting a warrior on horseback (See 192). The pattern marks the ground the horse walks on. Underneath, there crawls a chthonic beast – a dragon (See 094). Similar stones are found mainly in Sweden. 7th c. [3. Fig. 107]

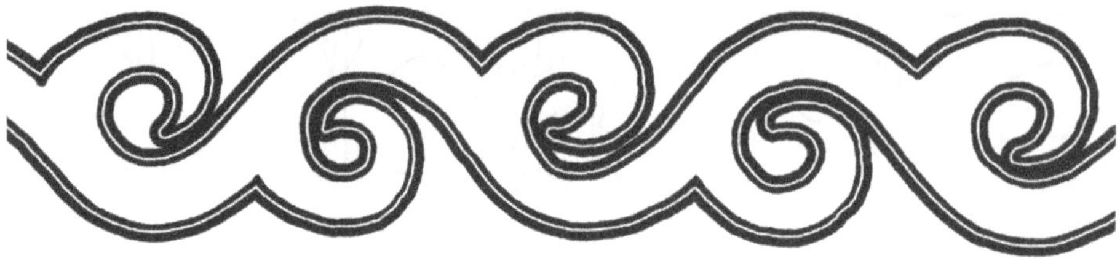

025 – Tendril pattern from a lower and upper guard of a sword from Grave V, Snartemo Hägebostad, Vest Agder, Norway. Early 6th c. (See 202) [Museum of Cultural History Oslo]

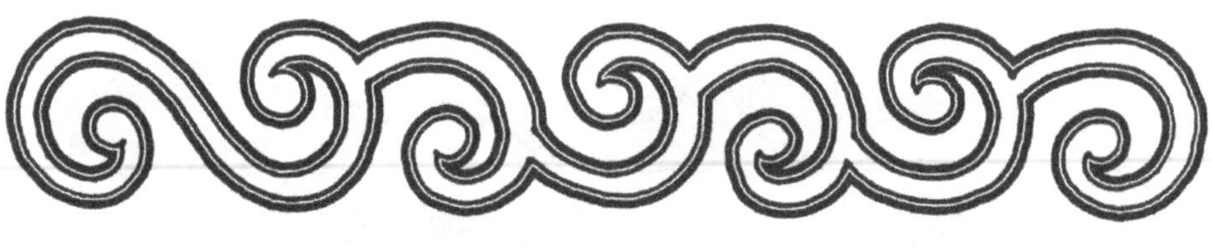

026 – Tendril pattern in Animal Style I on a gilded silver square-headed brooch from an AngloSaxon woman's grave at Chessell Down. The motif is present as a framed border on a rectangular head-plate (Also see 131) [17.16]

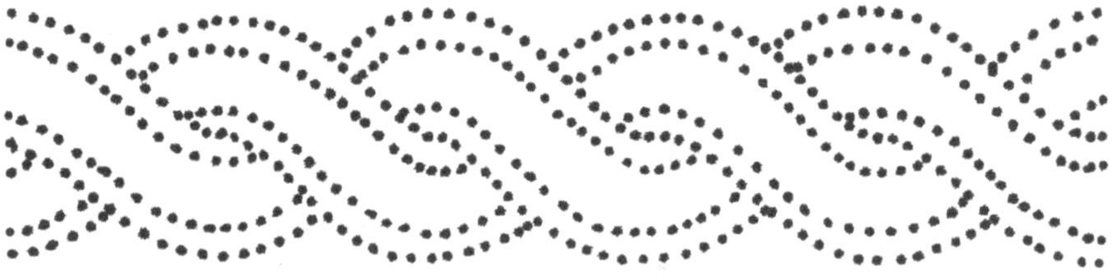

027 – Sunk ornament on a knife handle. Kylver, Gotland, ca. 550-600 CE [11. Table. 45, Fig. 473; 10.26, Fig. 473]

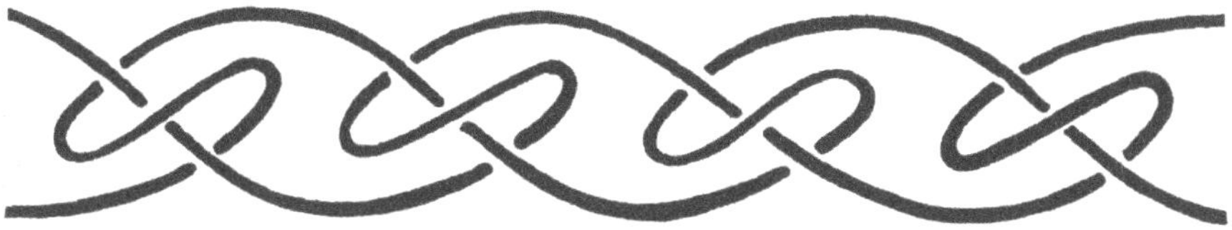

028 – One of the plaid ornaments on the hoop of a large fibula. Stora, Gotland, ca. 650- 700 CE. (Also see 032) [11.Table 164, Fig. 1372; 10.52, Fig. 1372]

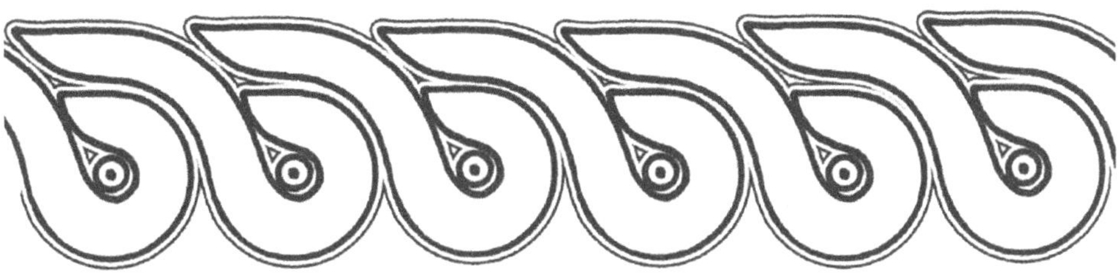

029 – Motif on the head plate of a gilded silver Ostrogoth bow fibula from the time of Theoderic the Great, 5th-6th c., Reggio Emilia, Italy (Also see 137) [12, dwg. 22]

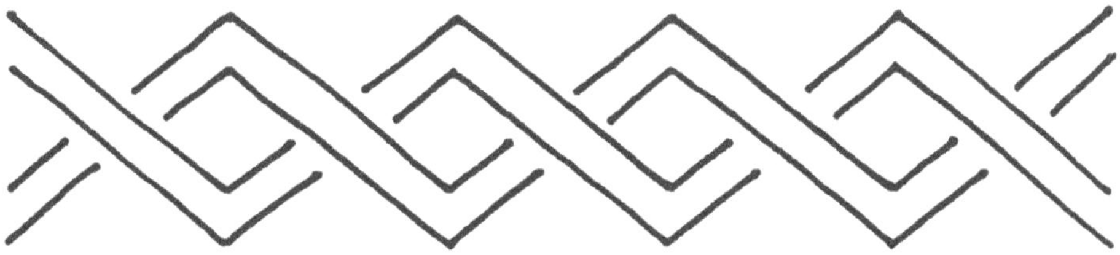

030 – Ornament on the rim of a middle part of a large fibula. Gotland, ca. 600-650 CE [11.Table 102, Fig. 862; 10.37, Fig. 862]

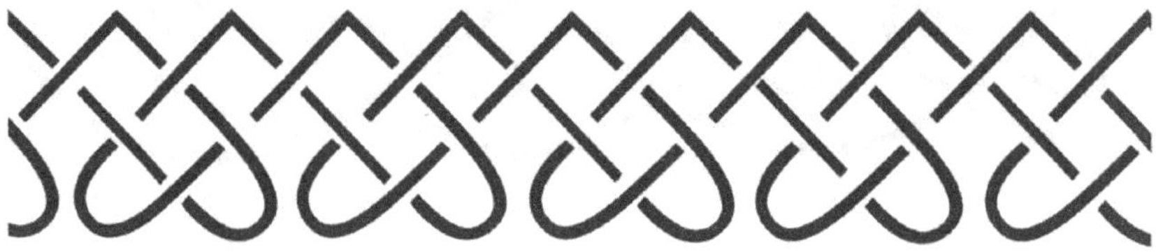

031 – Ornament on the rim of a large fibula. Stora, Gotland, ca. 650-700 CE. (Also see 037) [11.Table 162, Fig. 1370; 10.52, Fig. 1370]

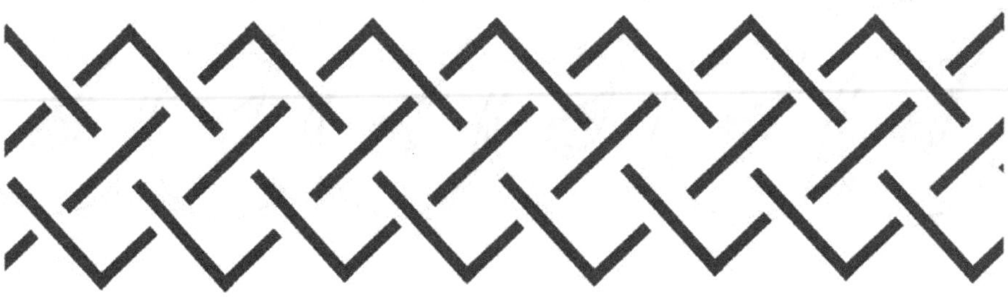

032 – See 028

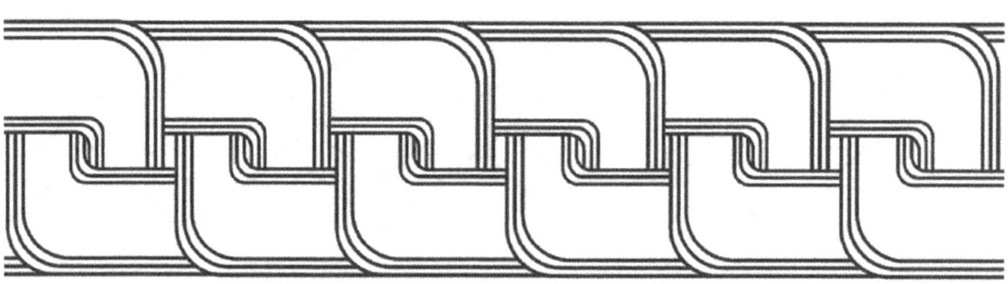

033 – Motif curved with a knife decorating the shaft of a spear from the Nydam Bog (Nydam III Horizon), 400-450 CE. Identical ornaments can be found in the bog deposits at Kragehul, we often find spear shafts decorated with interlacing, rope, plait, chain and scale patterns. Sometimes the plait patterns had elements which likened them to serpents. Denmark (Also see 041, 043, 50, 51) [6.p. 278-279. Fig.31; 9. p. 142]

034 – Plait ornament around the main triskelion motif (Also see 238) on a round fibula, Gotland, ca. 700-750 CE (Also see 149), [11.Table 221, Fig. 1812; 10.65, Fig. 1812]

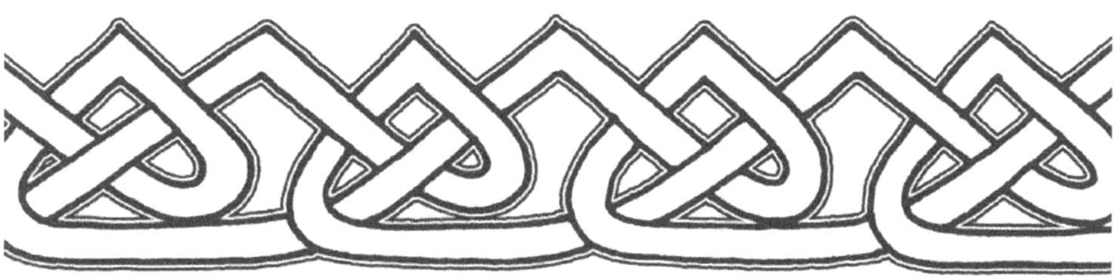

035 – Ornament on the rim of a round fibula. Gotland, ca. 650-700 CE, [11.Table. 168, Fig. 1398; 10.52-53, Fig. 1398]

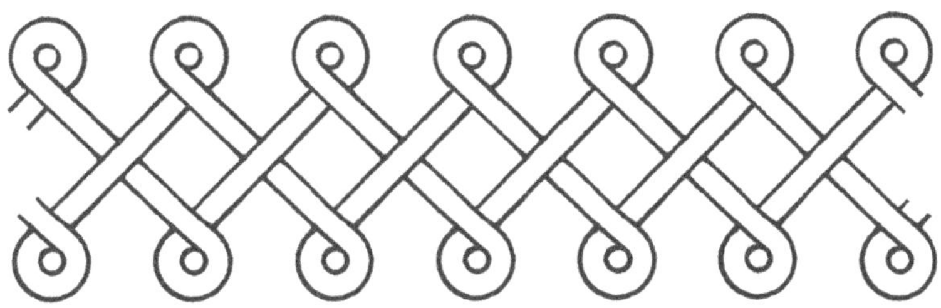

036 – Ornament on a large fibula. Gotland, ca. 650-700 CE, [11.Table. 160, Fig. 1366; 10.52, Fig. 1366]

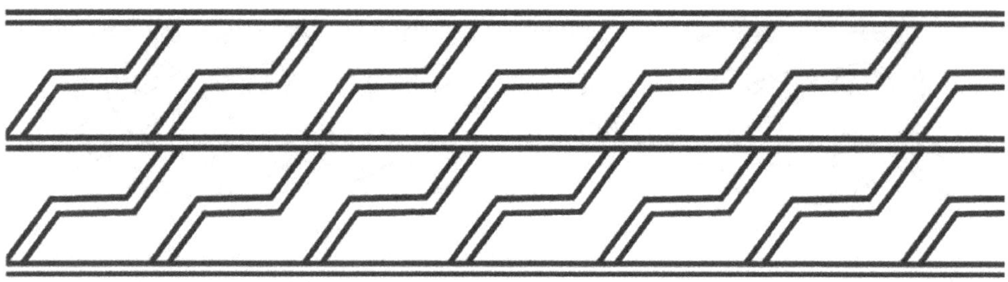

037 – Motif on the main plate of the fibula described under No. 031

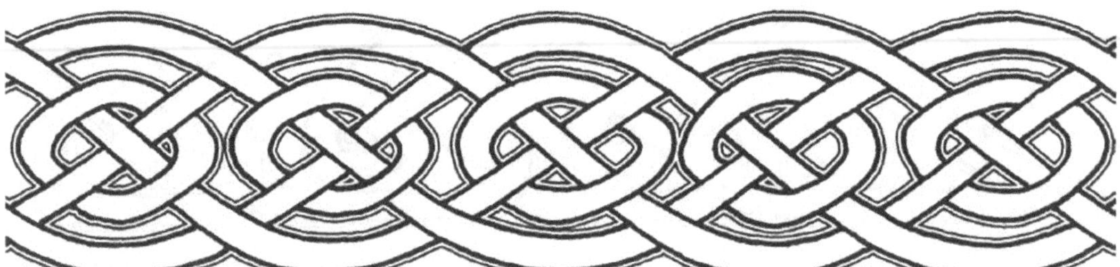

038 – Plait ornament from a bronze fibula fragment. Gotland, ca. 700-750 CE, [11.Table. 220, Fig. 1804; 10.65, Fig. 1804]

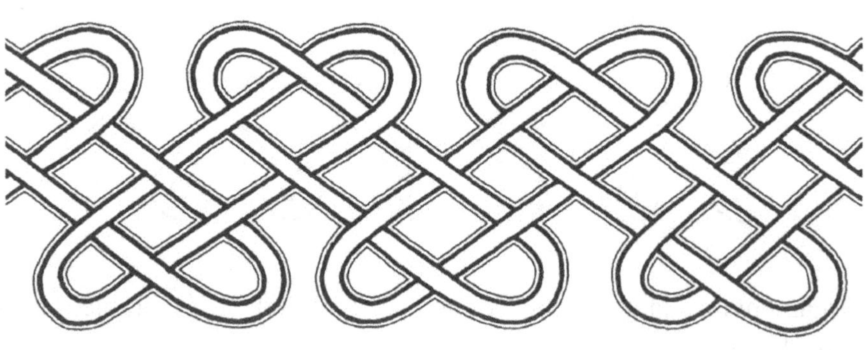

039 – Plait ornament from a bronze fibula. Gotland, ca. 700-750 CE, [11.Table. 220, Fig. 1800; 10.65, Fig. 1800]

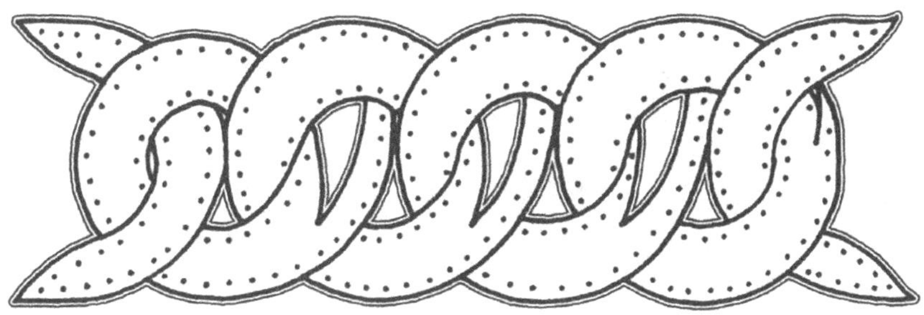

040 – Motif on a north-Germanic gilded, silver fibula from Foss, Amt Lyngdal, Vest-Agder, Norway, 6th c. [3, Fig. 47]

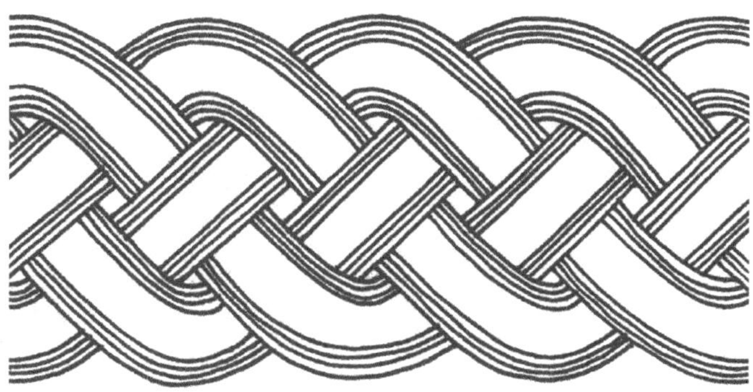

041 – Motif curved with a knife decorating the shaft of a spear from the Nydam Bog (Nydam IV Horizon), still the Kragehul style, similar to the earlier Nydam III specimens. Denmark (Also see 033, 043, 50, 51) [6.238]

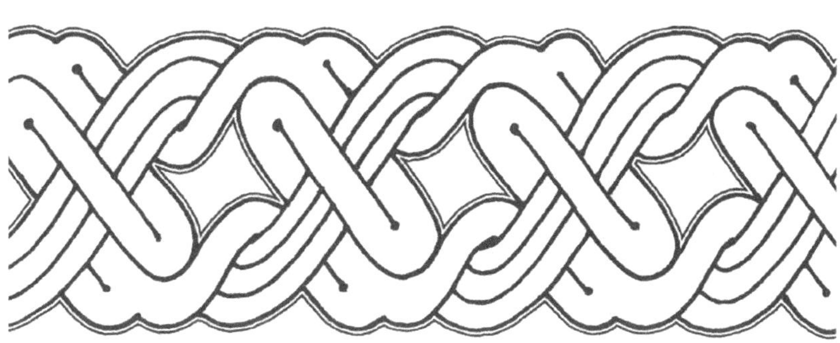

042 – Animal Style II ornament on a rectangular bronze, gilded belt strap plate. Gotland, ca. 550-600 CE [11. Table 30, Fig. 327; 10.21, Fig. 327]

043 – Plait motif from the shaft of a spear from the Kragehul bog, Denmark. 5th c. (Also see 033, 041, 50, 51) [9.142]

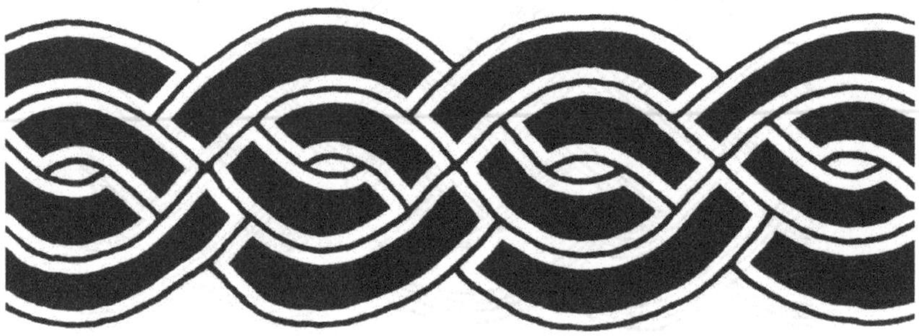

044 – Animal Style II ornament on a rectangular bronze gilded belt strap plate. Gotland, ca. 550-600 CE [11. Table 30, Fig. 329; 10.21, Fig. 329]

045 – Filigree ornament on the golden pommel of a sword found in Wellingore, Buckingamshire, England, 8th c. [9.109]

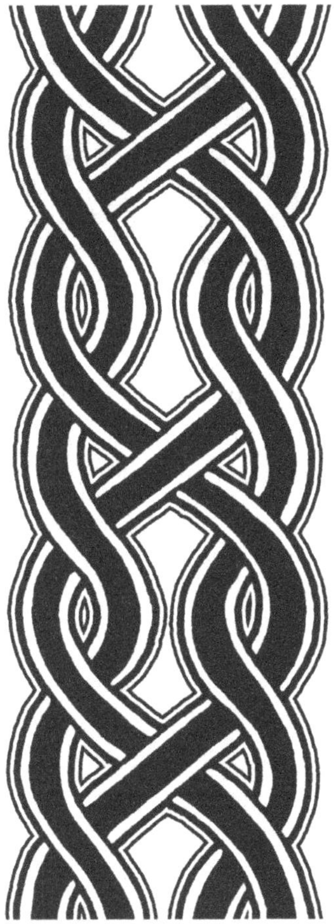

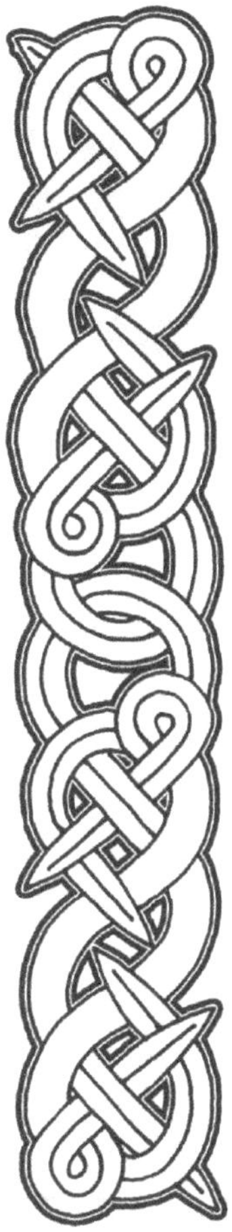

046 (left) – Animal Style II ornament on a rectangular bronze gilded belt strap plate. Gotland, ca. 550-600 CE [11. Table 30, Fig. 328; 10.21, Fig. 328]

047 (right) – Interlacing pattern, Style II, die-embossed on a tinned bronze plate, the so-called pressbleck, of a helmet from the royal Mound 1 ship burial in Sutton Hoo, belonging one of the kings of East Anglia, probably Raedwald (d. approx. 624/625 CE). The ornamental style is almost identical with the one known from the Vendel (See: 059) and Valsgärde graves, which makes it possible that it was made by a Swedish craftsman working for the East Anglian court. There is evidence that the most famed craftsmen traveled, alone or with their sovereigns, between mansions to perform special orders for the ruling class, carrying their tools and dies for embossing decorative plates. (For other ornaments from Sutton Hoo, see 016, 053, 060, 071, 077, 079, 085, 086 , 088, 089, 091, 098, 105, 117, 153, 183, 185, 191, 201, 202, 240) [4.46-49, 114-115]

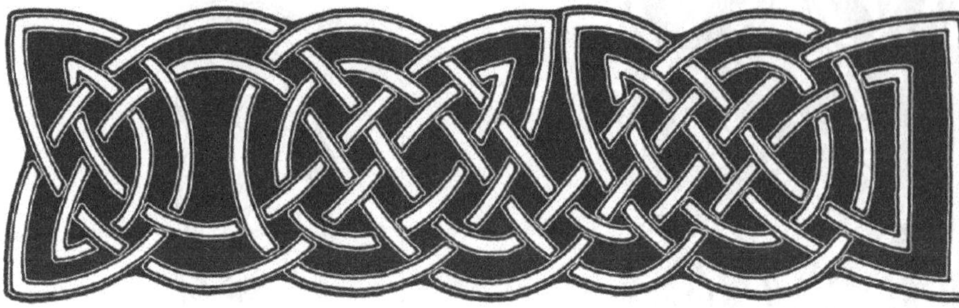

048 – Interlacing pattern on a wooden binding, front cover of the St Cuthbert Gospel of St. John, evidencing the connections between Britain and Ireland with the Near East, e.g. Coptic traditions, transferred by missionaries and travelers. Late 7th c. [17.110]

049 – Very late Animal Style II ornament on a long, approximately rectangular plate. It appeared in this period and was still found in Gotland throughout the Viking Age. Gotland, ca. 650-700 CE [11.Table 188, Fig. 1565; 10.57, Fig. 1565]

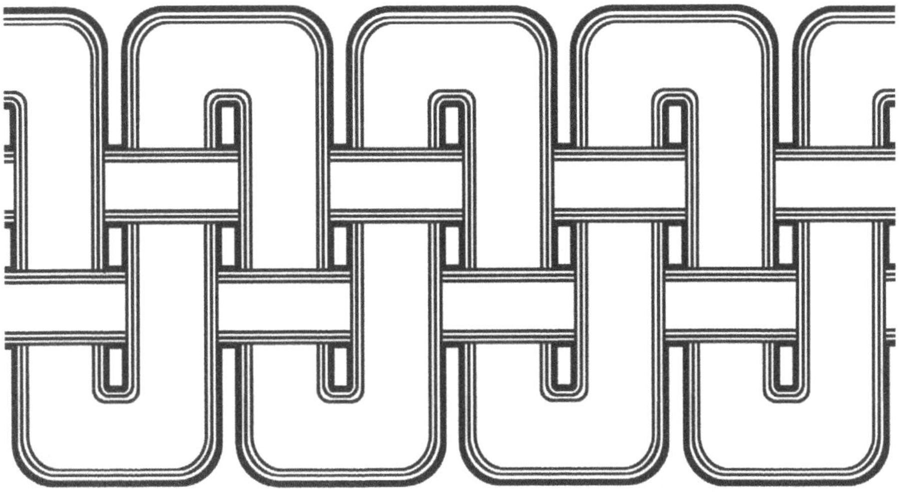

050 – Plait motif from the shaft of a spear from the Kragehul bog, Denmark. 5th c. (Also see 033, 041, 43, 51) [9. p. 142]

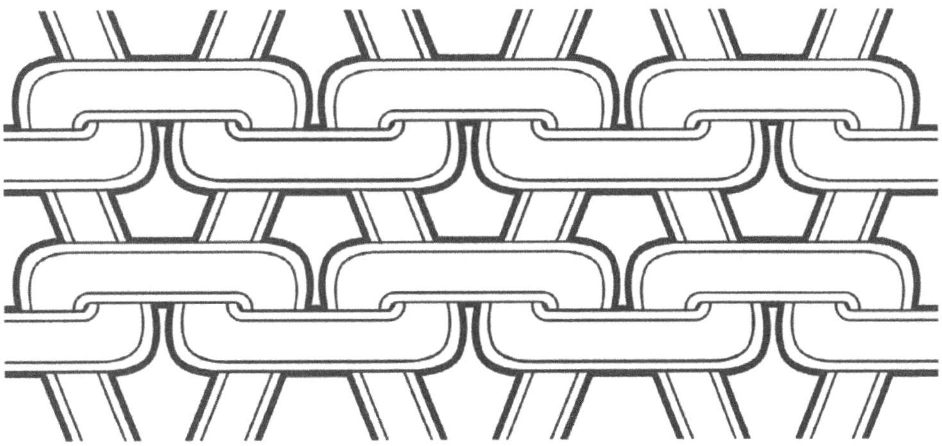

051 – as above.

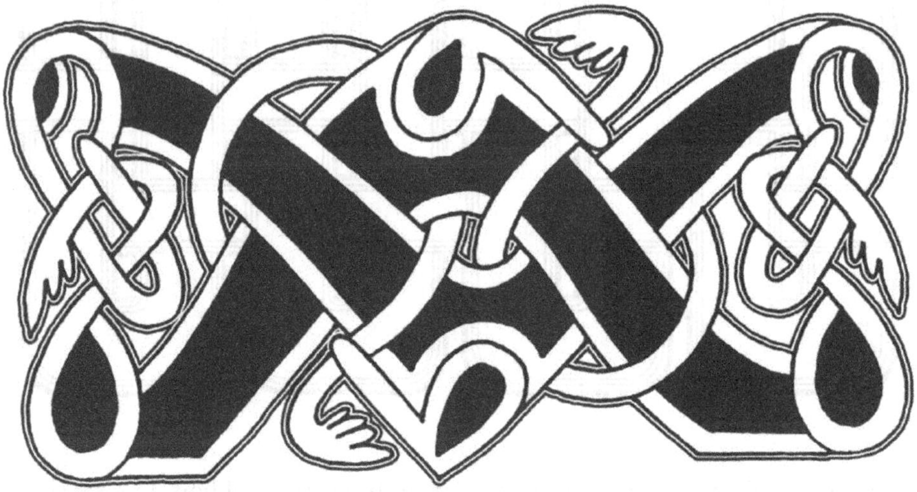

052 – Interlacing pattern from a bone plate from Southampton. Anglian version of Animal Style II which had originated in southern Scandinavia, in the second half of 7th c. and was transported via the continent to East Anglia. 6th-7th c. [17.62]

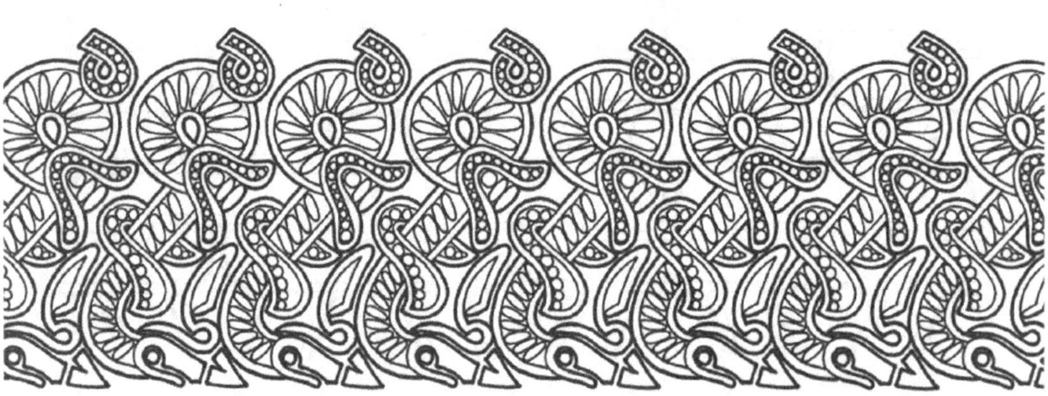

053 – Zoomorphic ornament adorning gilded, silver panels that make up the mouth fitting of the drinking horns from a Sutton Hoo burial (See 047) [4.64-66]

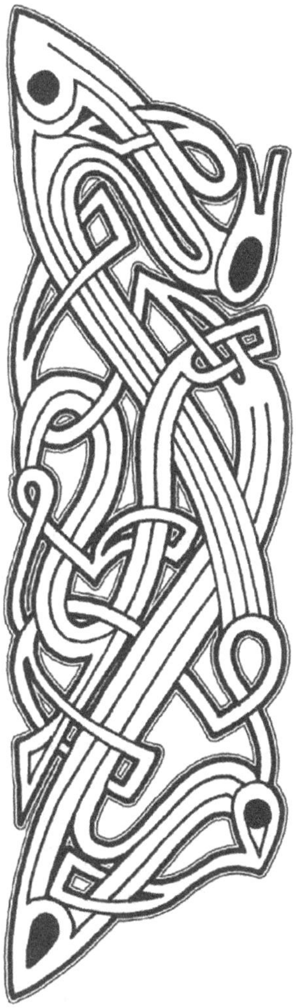

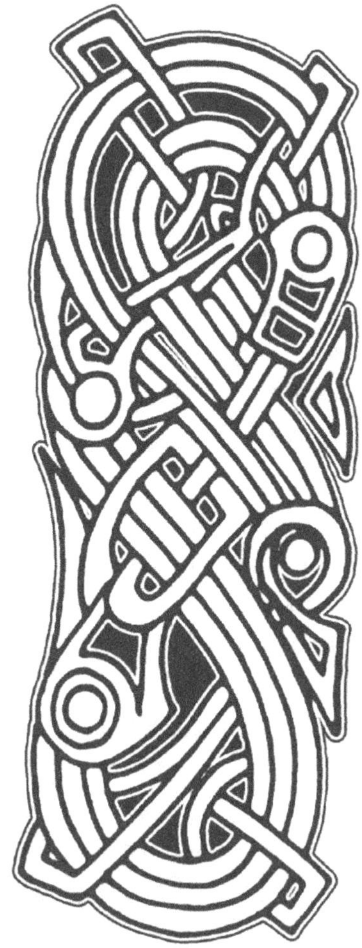

054 (left) – Zoomorphic ornament in the very late Animal Style II from the grip of a sword from Gotland, ca. 650-700 CE. (Also see 078) [11.Table 200, Fig. 1670a; 10.60-61, Fig. 1670a]

055 (right) – Animal Style II ornament on a rectangular plate. Gotland, ca. 650-700 CE [11.Table 190, Fig. 1580; 10.58, Fig. 1580]

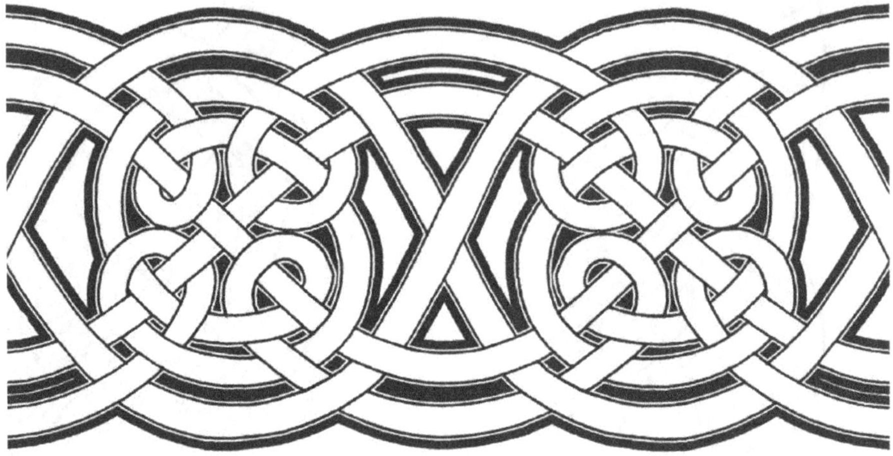

056 – Ribbon interlace on a curvilinear carpet page of the Book of Durrow. The book is an example manifesting that insular manuscripts included patterns used in metalworking both from the Anglo-Saxon and Celtic traditions. It is an early stage insular style, ca. 680 CE [17.103-105]

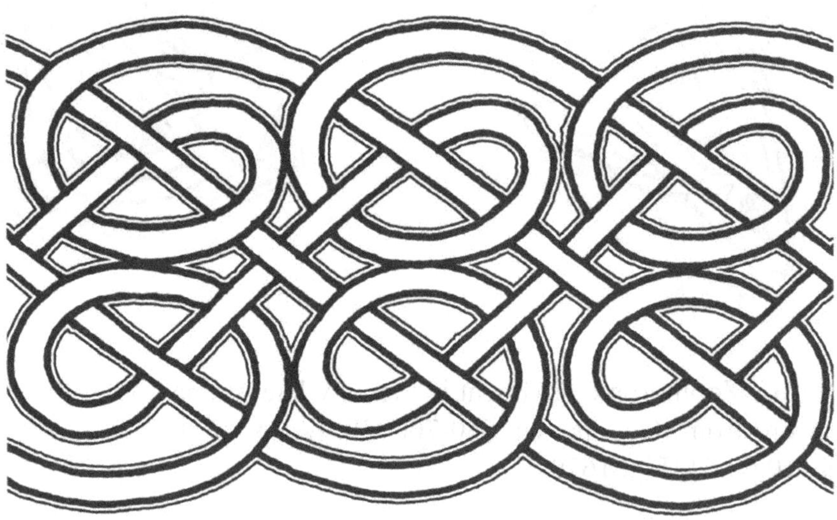

057 – Plait ornament from a bronze fibula fragment. Gotland, ca. 700-750 CE, [11.Table. 220, Fig. 1803; 10.65, Fig. 1803]

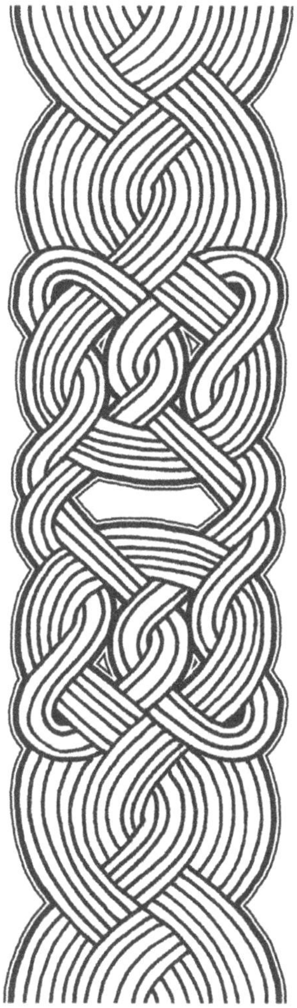

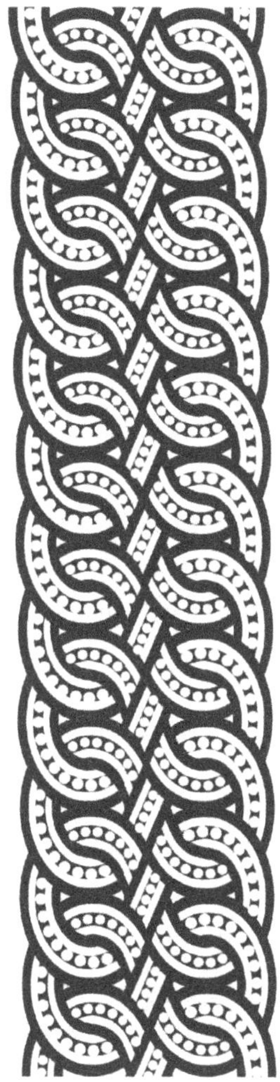

058 (Left) – Plait pattern on a bronze overlay on the iron fitting on a shield, Gotland, ca. 550-600 CE [11.Table 74, Fig. 658; 10.31, Fig. 658]

059 (Right) – Motif modeled on the plaid pattern on an embossed plate (the so-called pressblech) on the central rim of the helmet from the Vendel XIV grave at Vendel parish burial site, which was an element of an Uppsala öd complex, the political center of Sweden. It gave its name to the Scandinavian Iron Age that preceded the Viking Era: Vendel Era. 550-793 CE, Uppland, Sweden, late 6th c. (For other patterns from this burial site see No. 080) [9.51,66-67; 14.14-15]

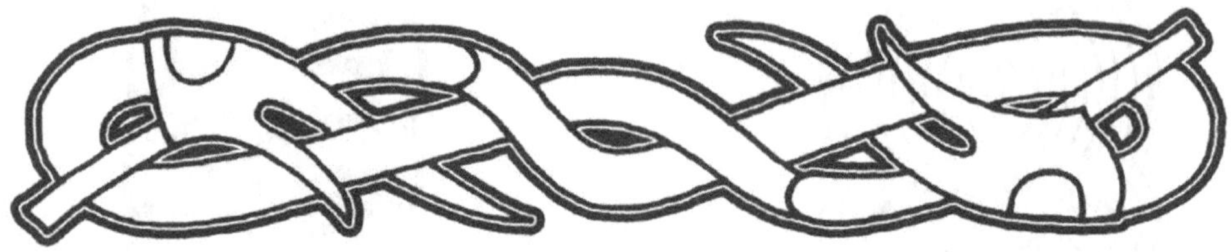

060 – Animal Style II ornament on golden shoulder-clasps from the Mound 1 ship burial at Sutton Hoo (For other details thereof see No. 071, 117, 153; for information on this burial see No. 047) [4.87 and Plate VI; 1. Plate 1; 17.62]

061 – Zoomorphic ornament in early Animal Style II on the belt strap end from a man's burial. Gotland, ca. 550-600 CE. (Also see 078) [11.Table 24, Fig. 262; 10.20, Fig. 262]

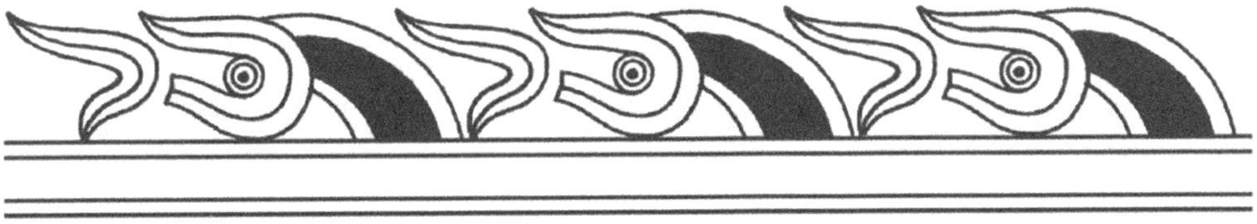

062 – Animal heads in early Animal Style II on the outer rim of a large, semicircular rivet – an element in the rim of a shield. Gotland, ca. 550-600 CE [11.Table 75, Fig. 668; 10.31, Fig. 668]

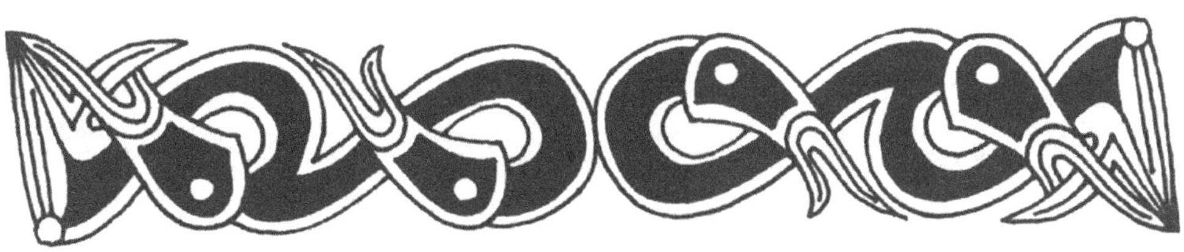

063 – Early Animal Style II ornament on a rectangular bronze, gilded belt strap plate. Gotland, ca. 550-600 CE [11.Table 29, Fig. 321; 10.21, Fig. 321]

064 – Zoomorphic ornament in early Animal Style II from the belt strap end from a man's burial. Gotland, ca. 550-600 CE. [11.Table 24, Fig. 264; 10.20, Fig. 264]

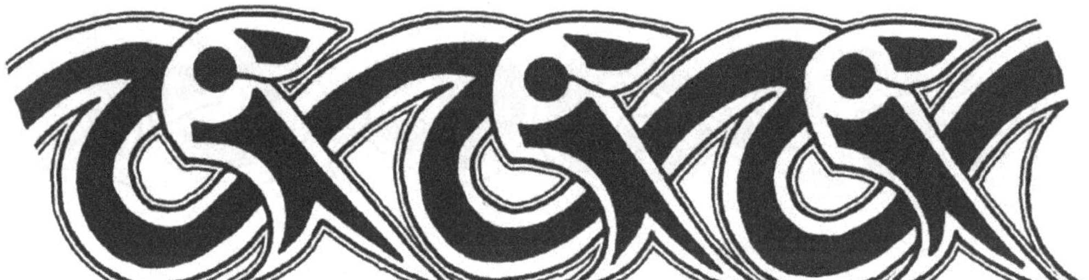

065 – Mature Animal Style II pattern on the iron fitting on a shield. Gotland, ca. 600-650 CE [11.Table 143, Fig. 1247; 10.47, Fig. 1247]

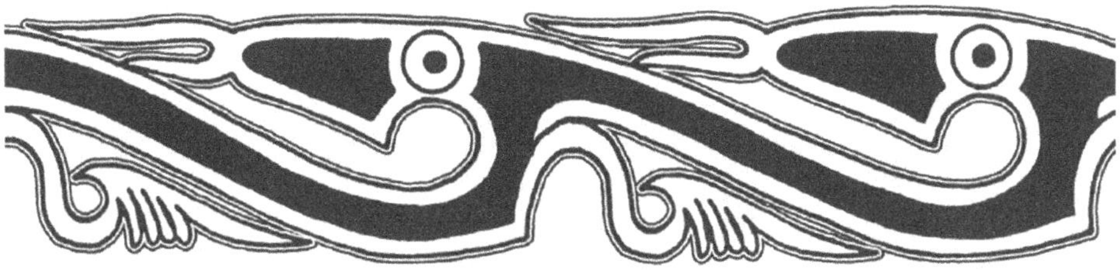

066 – Zoomorphic ornament on the bronze overlay of the rim of a shield boss (Also see 135). Gotland, ca. 600-650 CE [11.Table 142, Fig. 1239; 10.47, Fig. 1239]

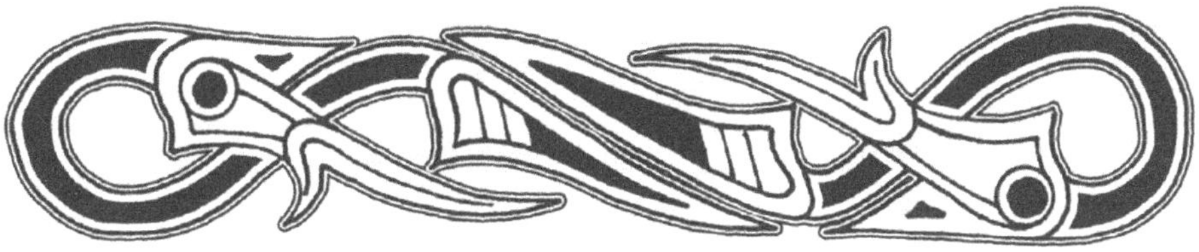

067 – Early Animal Style II ornament on a rectangular belt strap plate. Gotland, ca. 550-600 CE [11.Table 29, Fig. 318; 10.21, Fig. 318]

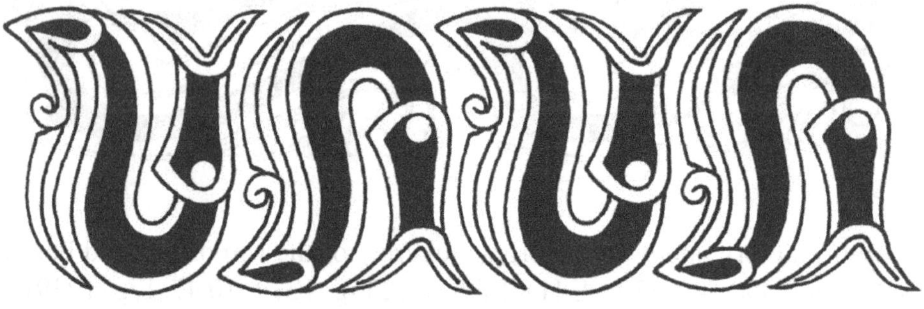

068 – Mature Animal Style II ornament on a rectangular bronze, gilded belt strap plate. Gotland, ca. 600-650 CE [11.Table 119, Fig. 1057; 10.42, Fig. 1057]

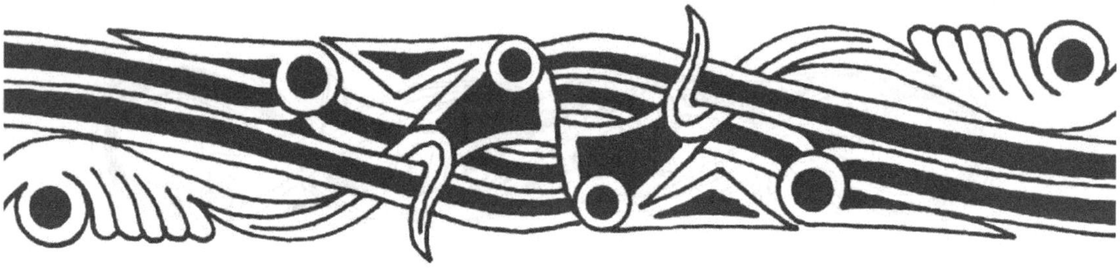

069 – Early Animal Style II ornament on a rectangular belt strap plate. Gotland, ca. 550-600 CE [11.Table 29, Fig. 319; 10.21, Fig. 319]

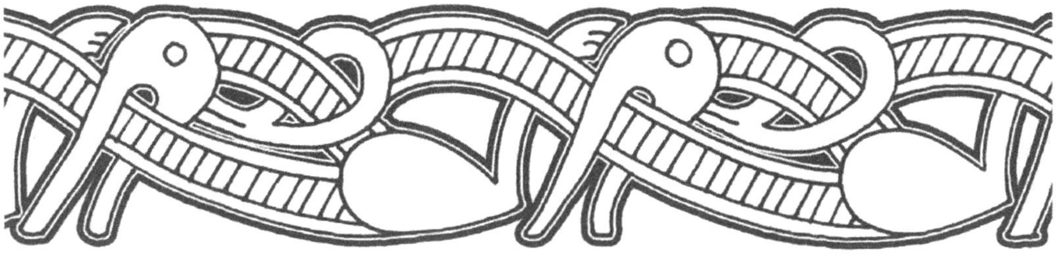

070 – Zoomorphic ornament on a large fibula. Gotland, ca. 650-700 CE, [11.Table. 165, Fig. 1373; 10.52, Fig. 1373]

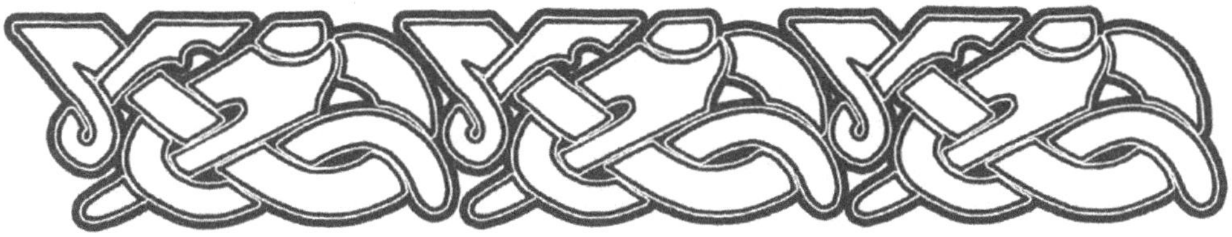

071 – Another detail of the Anglian Style II on the ornament described under No. 060

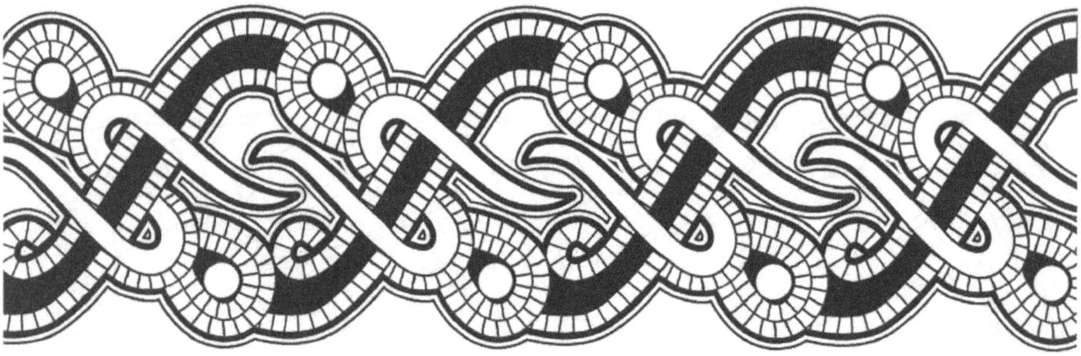

072 – Animal Style II pattern on a bronze overlay plate on the iron fitting on a shield. Gotland, ca. 550-600 CE [11.Table 74, Fig. 657; 10.31, Fig. 657]

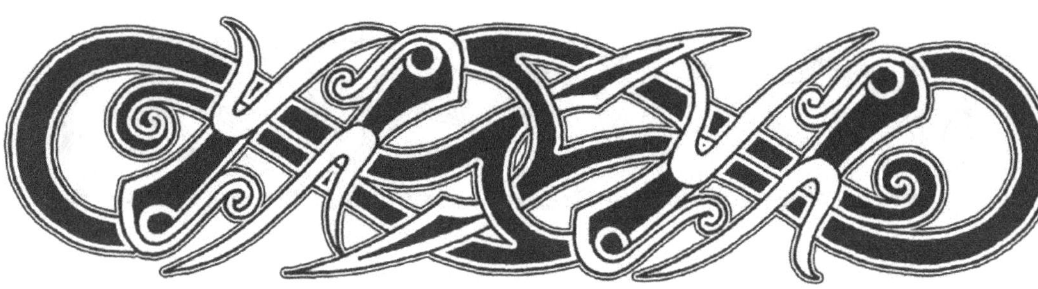

073 – Mature Animal Style II ornament on a rectangular bronze, gilded belt strap plate. Gotland, ca. 600-650 CE [11.Table 119, Fig. 1056; 10.42, Fig. 1056]

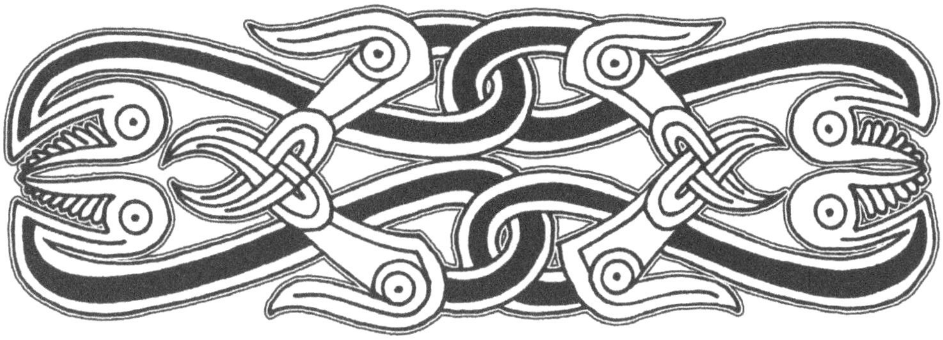

074 – Early Animal Style II ornament on a rectangular belt strap plate. Gotland, ca. 550-600 CE [11.Table 29, Fig. 325; 10.21, Fig. 325]

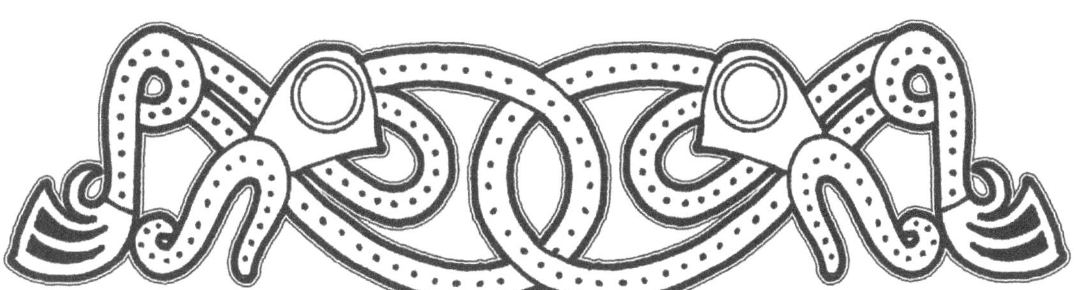

075 – Zoomorphic motif from a gilded guard of a ting-pommel sword. Originally, carbuncles were set as the eyes of the monster. Vallstenraunm, Gotland, ca. 600 CE [3. dwg. 146]

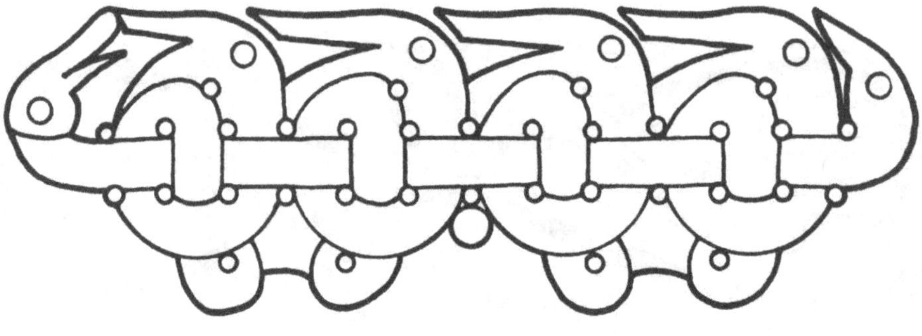

076 – Later Animal Style II ornament on a plate on a sheath. Gotland, ca. 650-700 CE [11.Table 201, Fig. 1675a; 10.21, Fig. 1675]

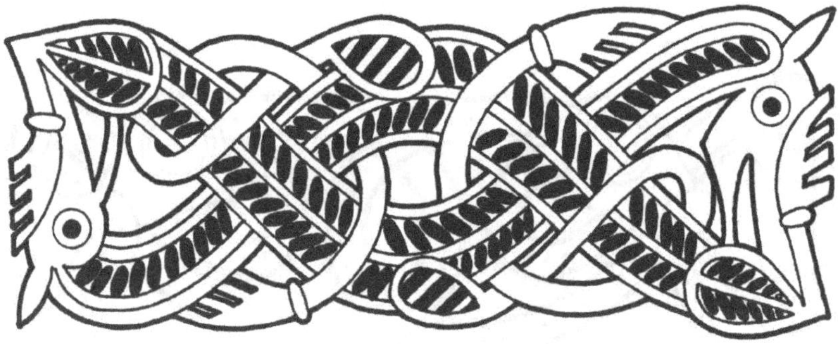

077 – Zoomorphic ornament on a plate on the neck of a maple wood bottle from Mound 1 ship burial at Sutton Hoo (for more information on this burial see 047) [17.123, dwg. 81]

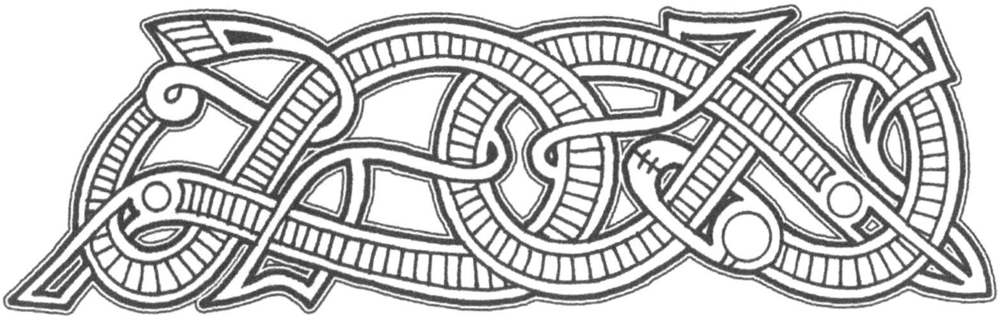

078 – Zoomorphic ornament in the very late Animal Style II on the grip of a sword from Gotland, ca. 650-700 CE. (Also see No. 054) [11.Table 200, Fig. 1670b; 10.60-61, Fig. 1670b]

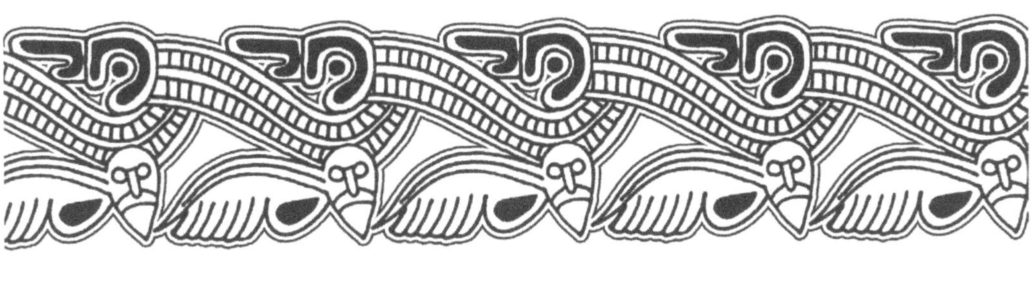

079 – Ornament adorning gold foil plaques. A wing of a bird of prey as a decorative fitting of a shield from the Mound 1 ship burial at Sutton Hoo (for information on the burial see No. 047, for another ornament from this shield see No. 088, and for the whole figure of the bird see No. 185), [4.49-55, Fig. 35]

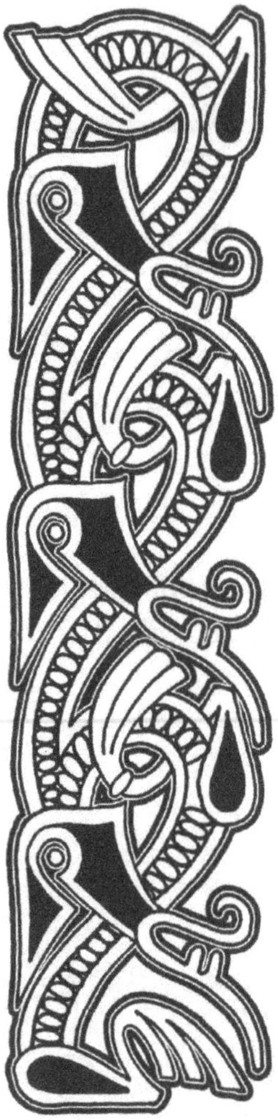

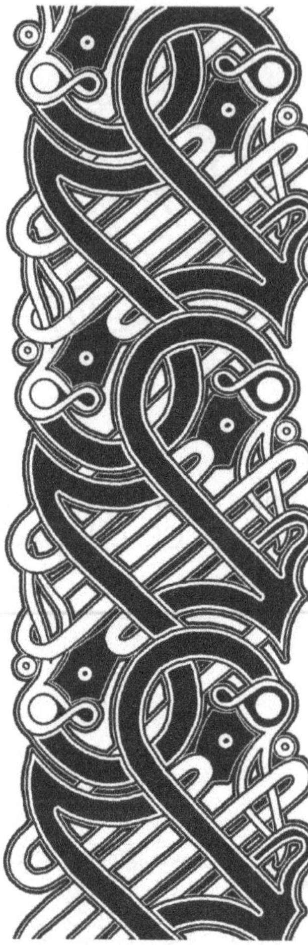

080 (left) – Zoomorphic ornament on a pressblech from the helmet of Vendel XII burial. The style of the helmet and shield from this grave is particularly alike to the one known from Mound 1 ship burial at Sutton Hoo (See 047). (For information on this site see No. 059, for other patterns from this burial see No. 092). England, 6th-7th c. [9.58]

081 (right) – Zoomorphic ornament embossed on a pressblech of the helmet from the Valsgärde 5 grave. Valsgärde is the name of a farm in Sweden where the 6th-11th c. burial site was discovered. Located in the immediate vicinity of Old Uppsala (Gamla Uppsala) which was the political and religious center of the Yngling Pagan rulers of Sweden (For other motifs on the same helmet see No. 083, and 097; for information on the site see No. 084), 7th c. [9.56]

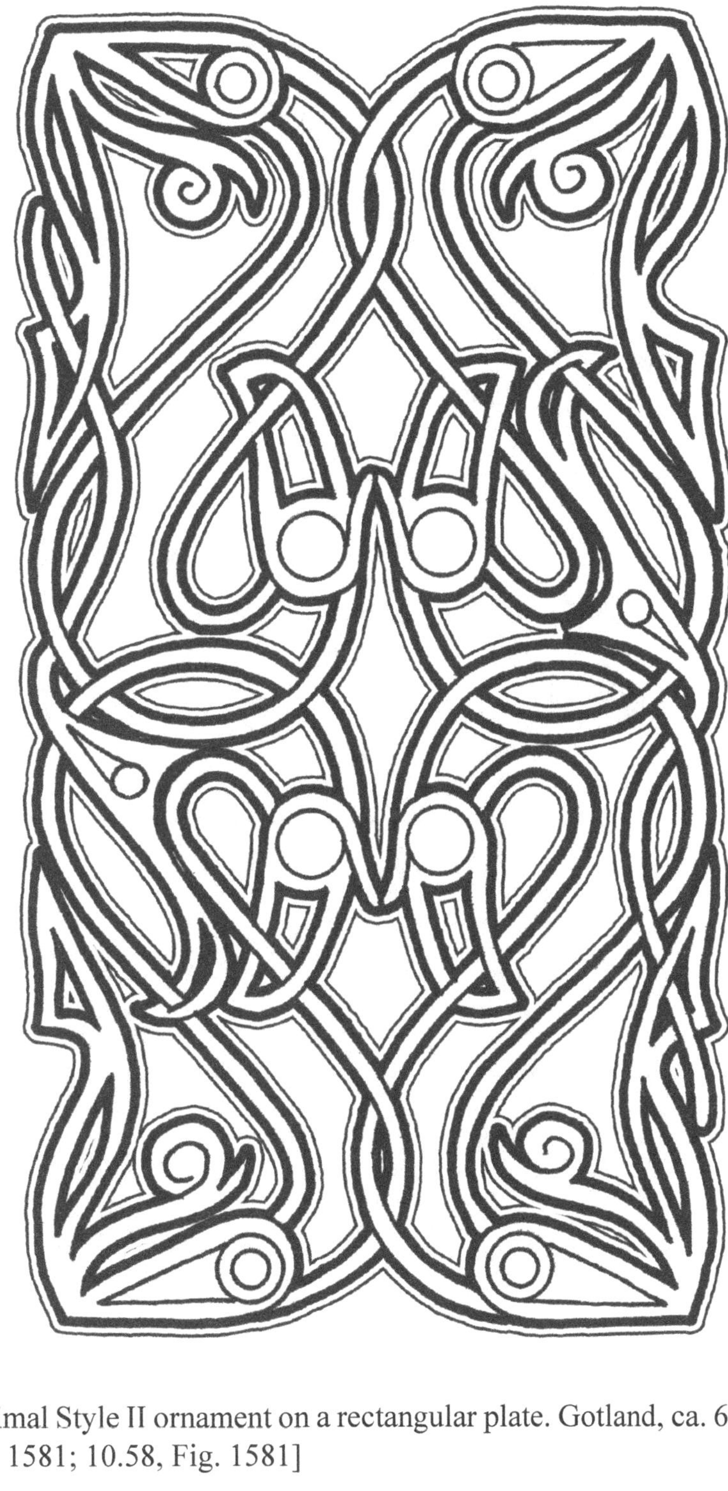

082 – Later Animal Style II ornament on a rectangular plate. Gotland, ca. 650-700 CE [11. Table 190, Fig. 1581; 10.58, Fig. 1581]

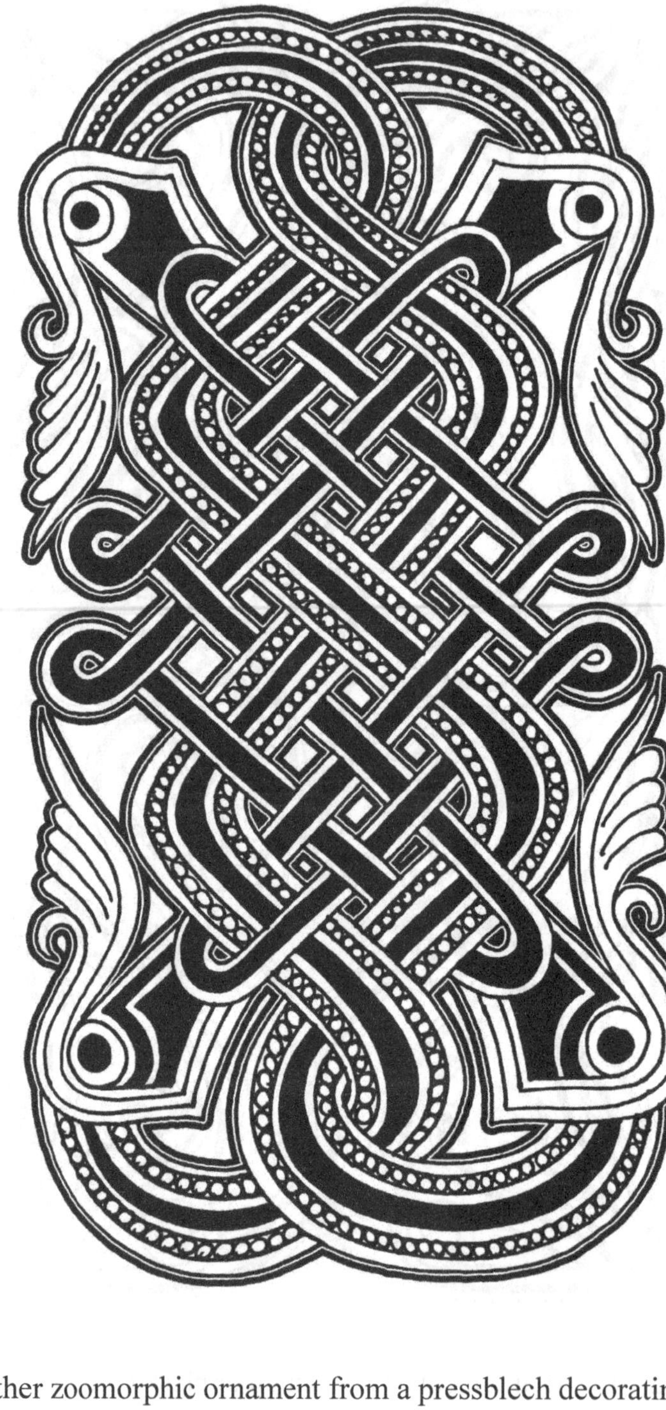

083 (right) – Another zoomorphic ornament from a pressblech decorating the Valsgärde 5 helmet (See 081, 097) [9.32, 56, 74]

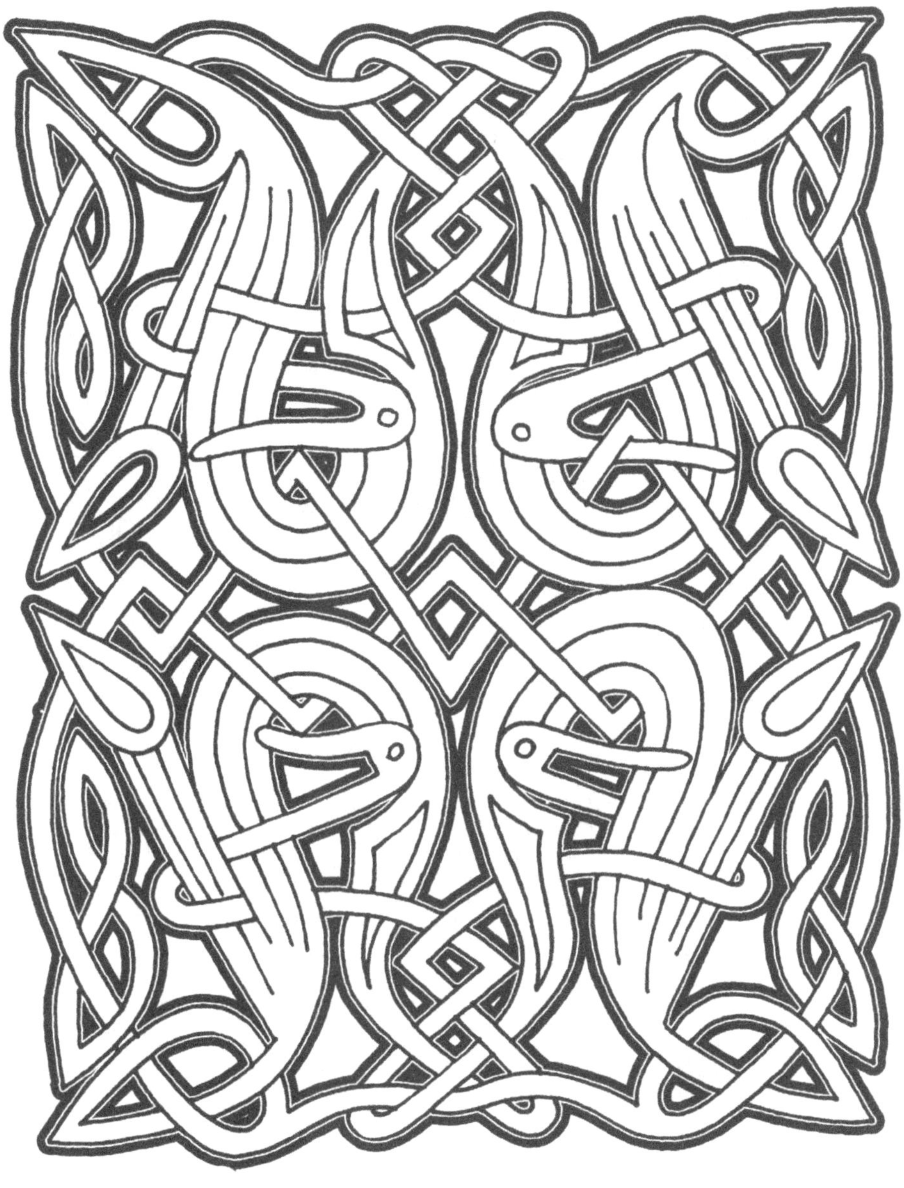

084 – Zoomorphic ornament from a pressblech decorating the Valsgärde 6 helmet (For information on the burial site see 081, for other motifs see 083) [2, 56, 74] 7th c. [9.31]

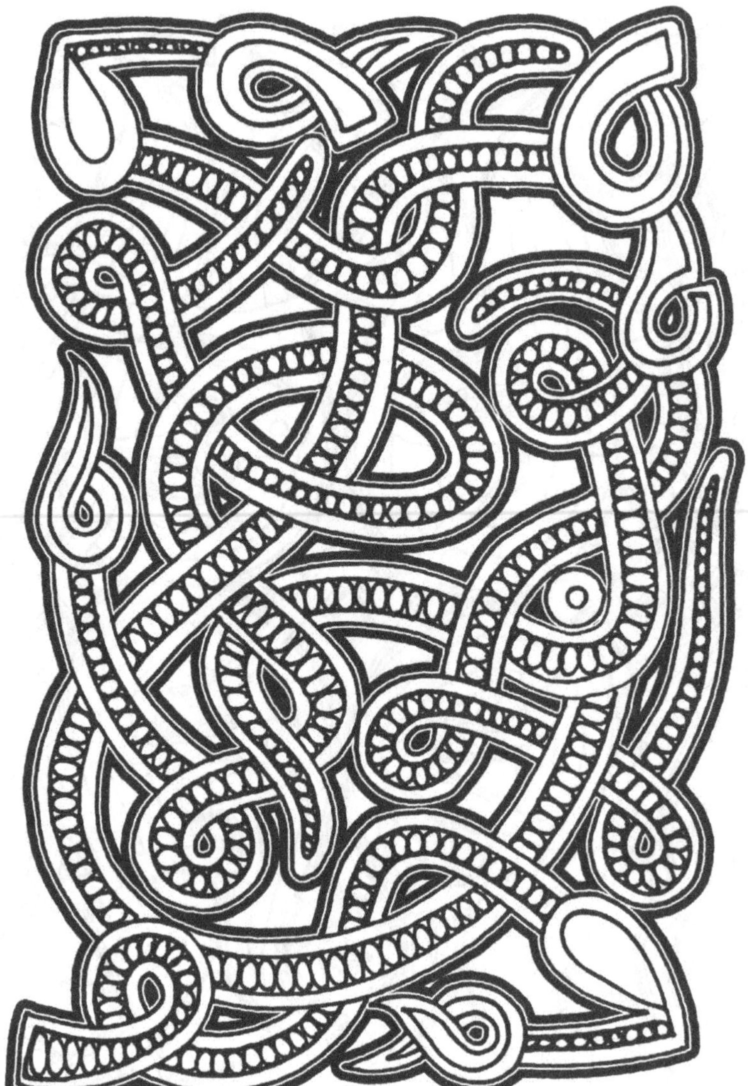

085 – Ornament on embossed pressblech of the helmet from Mound 1 ship burial at Sutton Hoo (See 047) [4.47]

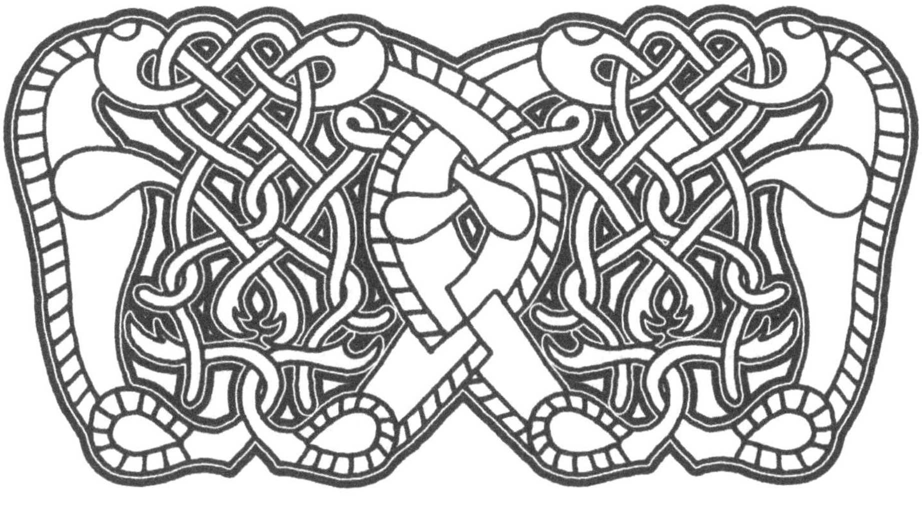

086 – Four interlacing animals on one of the seven golden decorative plaques on the purse lid from Sutton Hoo (see 047). These ornaments are a stylistic set is complemented by shoulder-clasps described under No. 060 (For other patterns from the purse see 183, 201) [4.87-88, plate VIII]

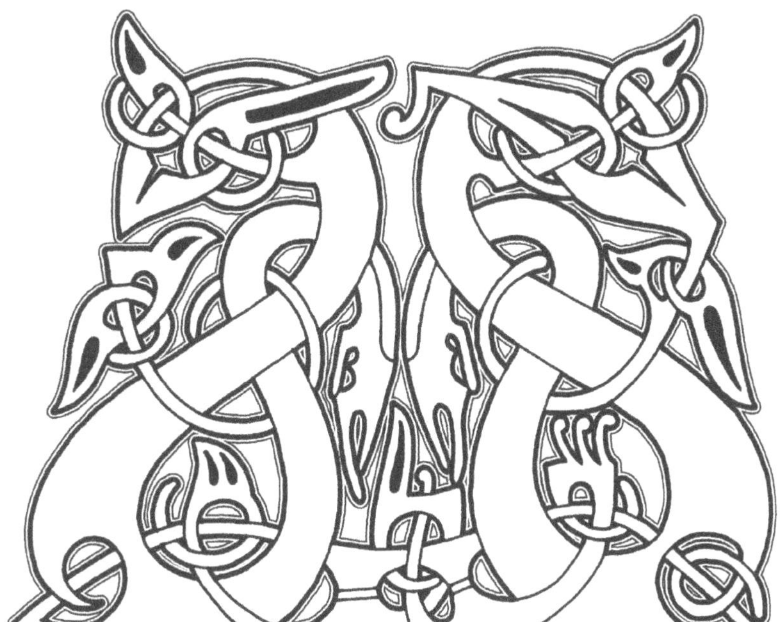

087 – Detail from the ornament on the large fibula classified as late Style III and early Carolingian style. Ca. 750-800 CE [11.Table 265, Fig. 2146; 10.76-77, Fig. 2146]

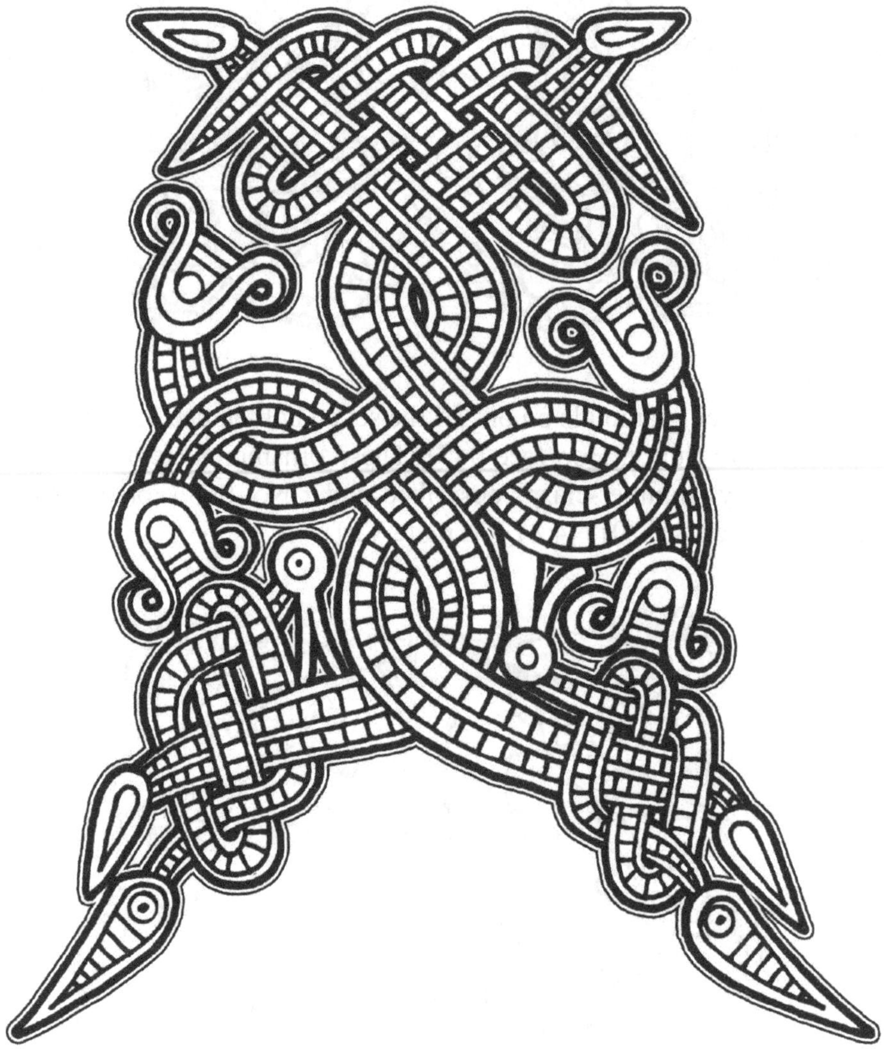

088 – Plait pattern on the tail of the bird depicted under No. 185 (For another ornament from this find, see No. 079) [4.49-55, Fig. 35]

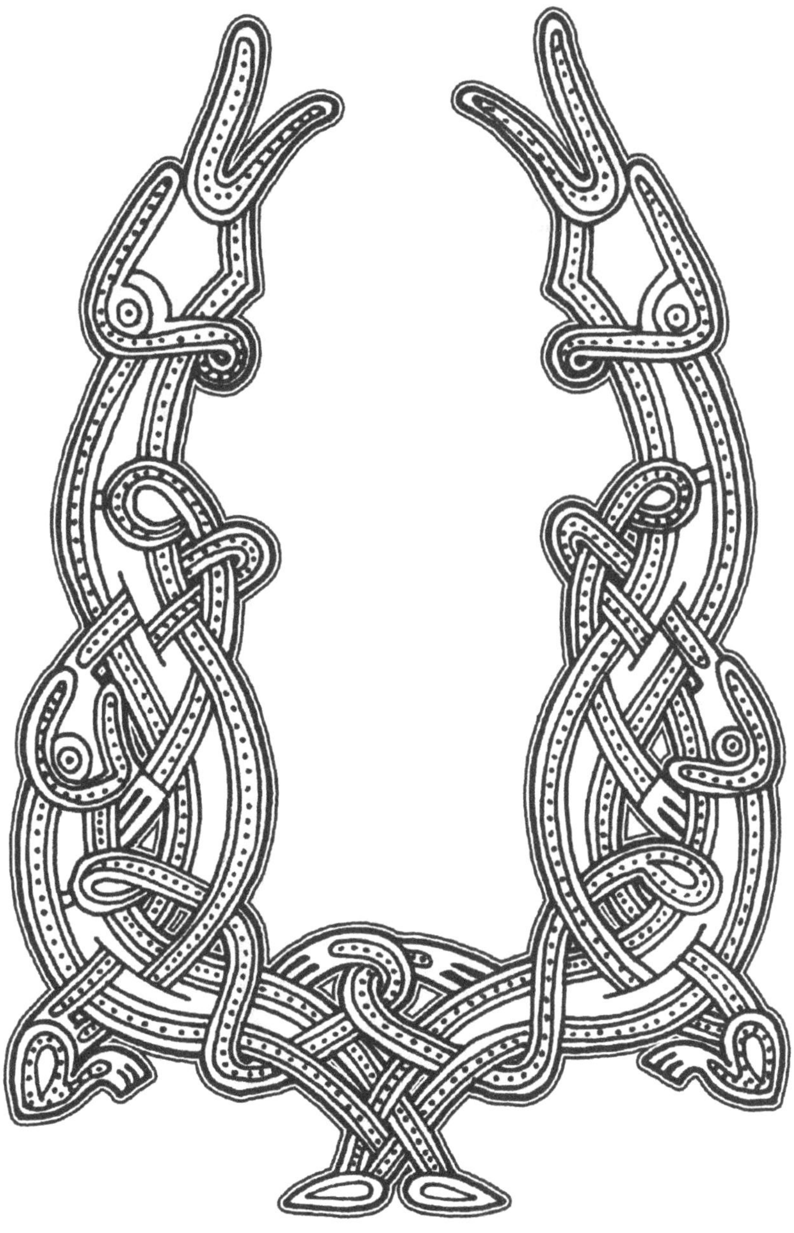

089 – Pattern with interlacing animals in Style II, on a large gold buckle from the grave at Sutton Hoo (see 047). The interior parts of the ornament are filled by the pattern depicted under No. 091. (For other details of the buckle, see No. 240) [17.64 -66, 1.11]

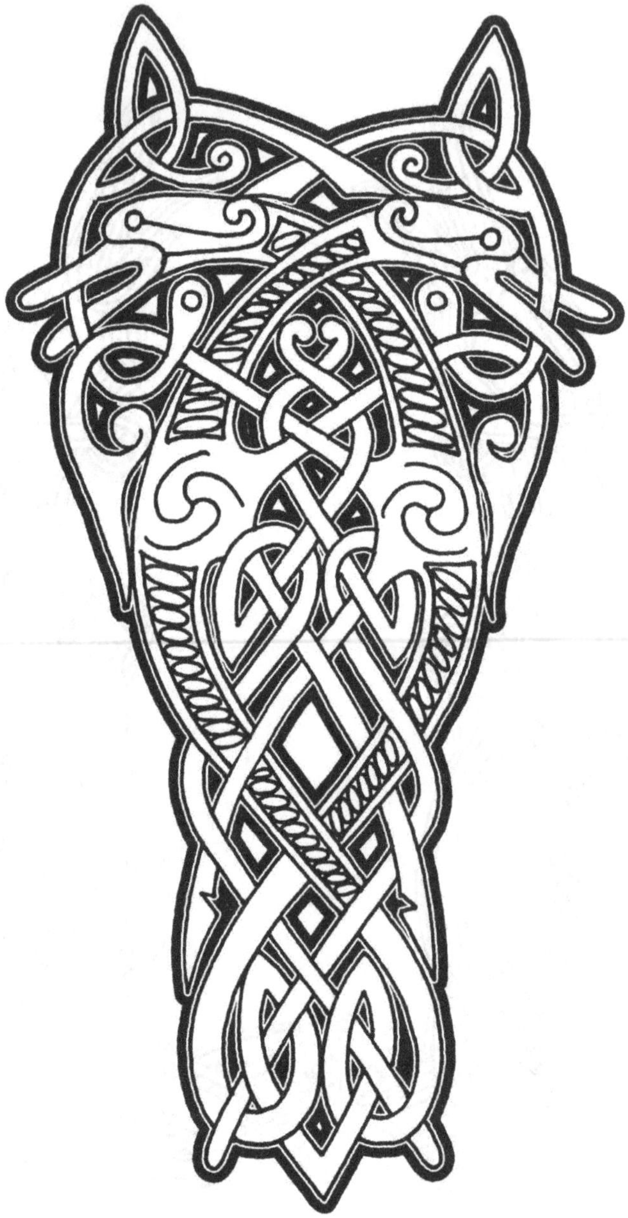

090 – Detail from the nasal part of the helmet from Coppergate, York. Other elements of the decorations point out that it belonged to a Christian warrior, however, the older Pagan traditions were still alive: representations of guardian animal heads and other beasts, coexist with the newer content. Later 8th c. [17.33]

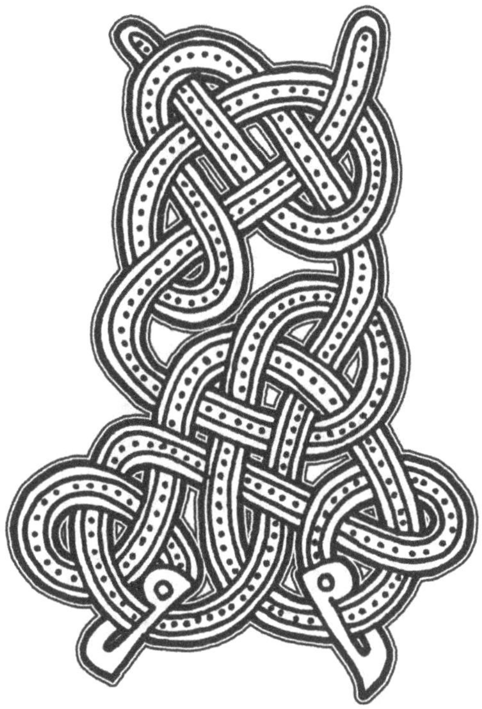

091 – Interlacing animals in Style II, filling the space inside the pattern presented in 089 [17.6466; 1.11]

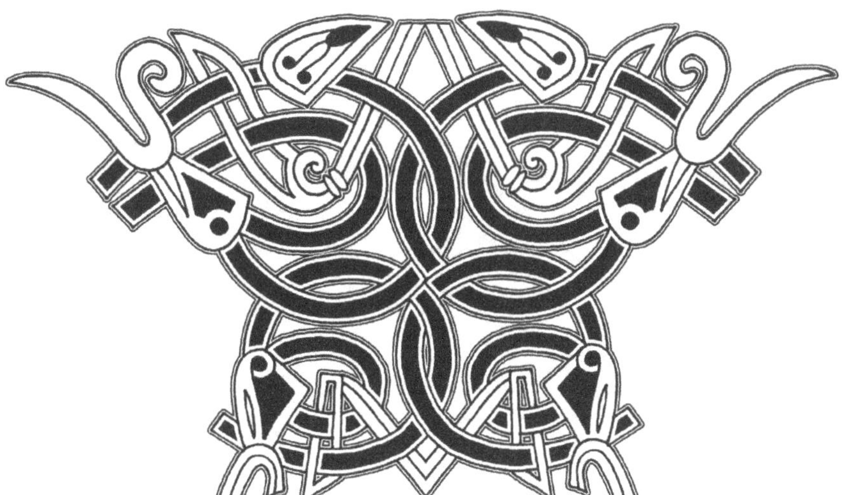

092 – Zoomorphic ornament on the flat part of the boss of the shield from the Vendel XII burial (See 080) [9.129]

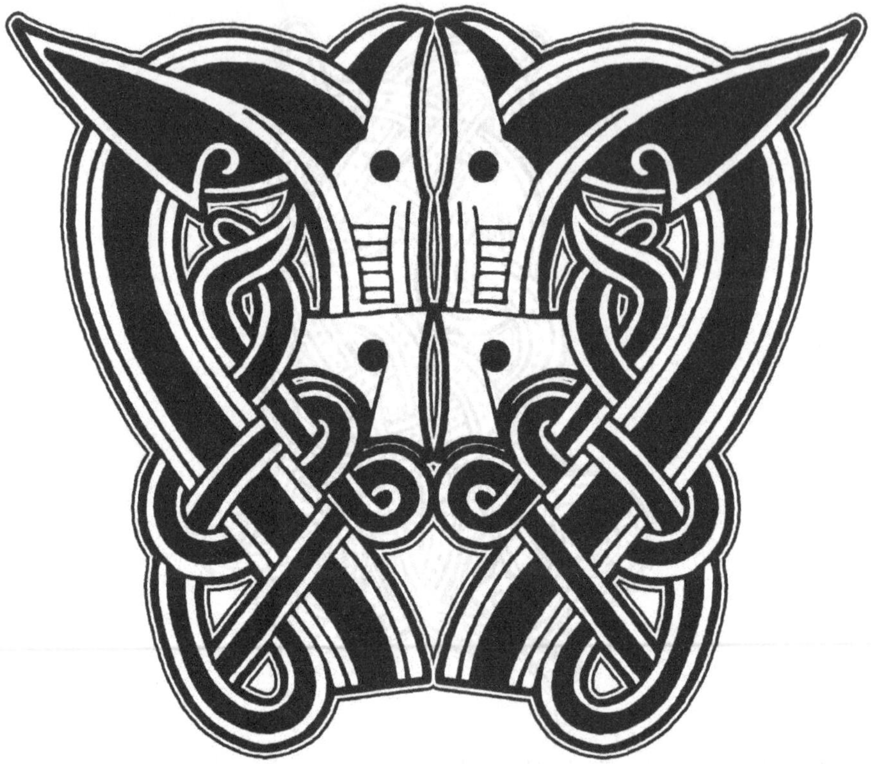

093 – Zoomorphic ornament on the flat part of the boss of the shield from the Vendel XI burial (For information on this site see No. 059, for another element of this boss see No. 119, also see No. 092) [9.128]

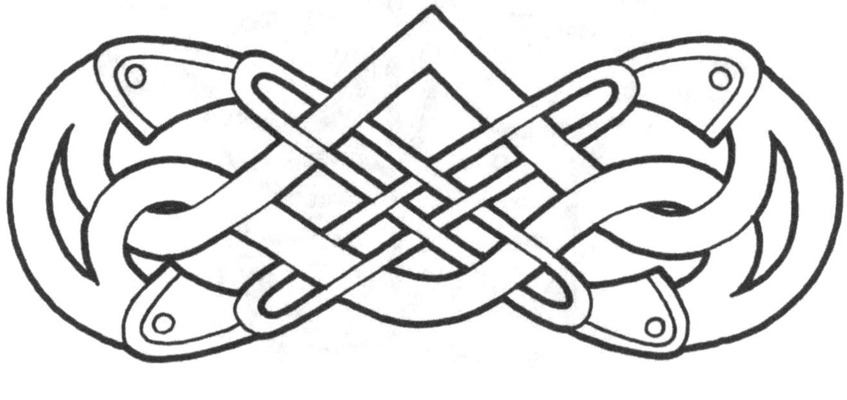

094 – Serpent-like, two-headed dragon, possibly a representation of the powers of the underworld, depicted on the Hornhausen stone. 7th c. For other details of the ornaments on this Stone see No. 024, and 192 [3. dwg. 107]

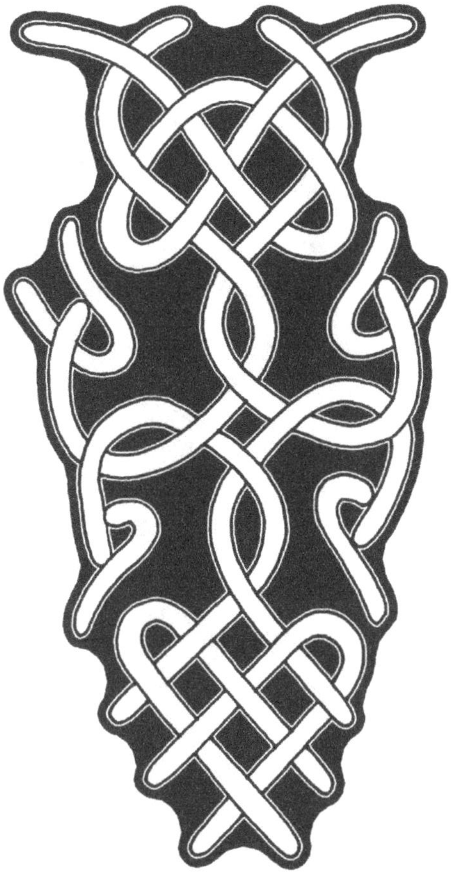

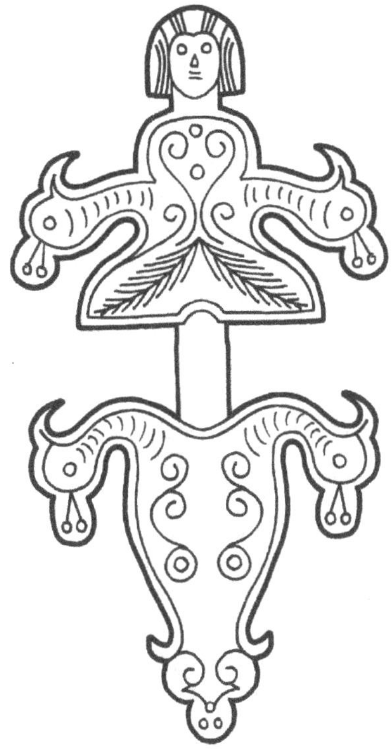

095 – Animal Style II ornament on gold-sheeted clasps from the princely burial at Taplow, Buckingamshire, early 7th c. [17.63-64]

096 – Silver fibula from the treasury of Martynivka (District of Kiev), Middle Dnieper. Brooches of this type are generally considered to represent the Universal Triad. This treasure, discovered in the land of the Slavic Antes, appears to be mix of Byzantine and Iranian influences. 7th c. (Also see 173) [British Museum, 16]

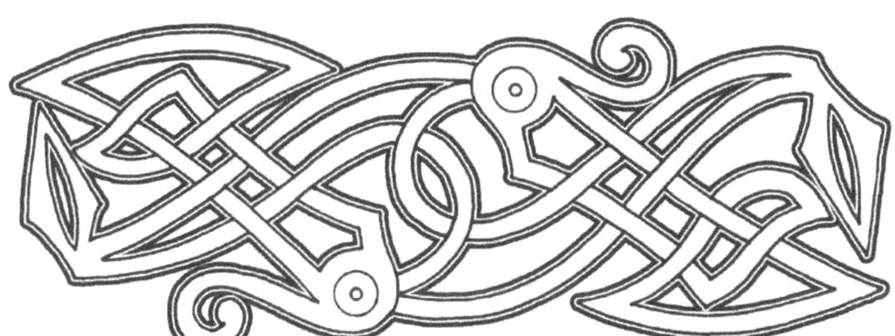

097 – Ornament embossed on the silver plate decorating the nasal part of the Valsgärde 5 helmet (See No. 081, 083) [9.32]

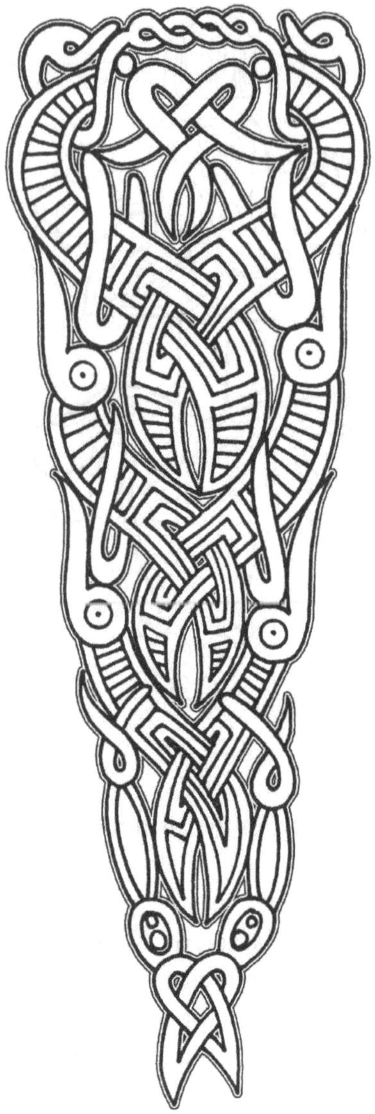

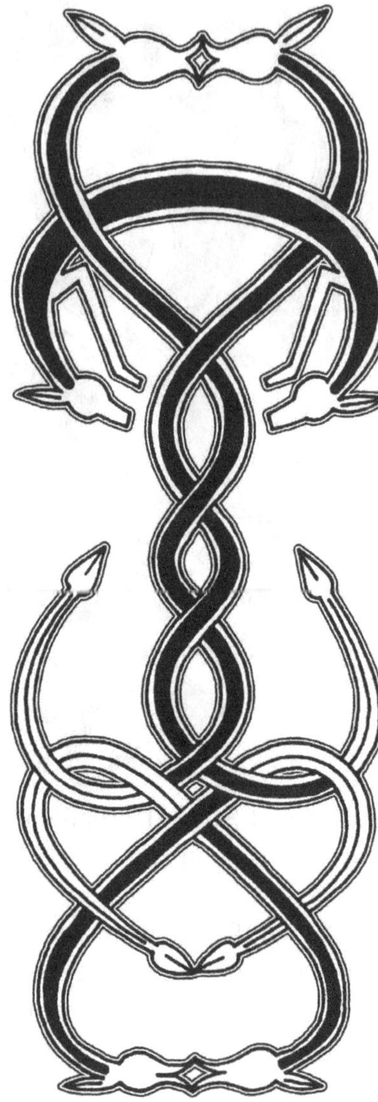

098 (left) – Zoomorphic ornament on gilded silver panels decorating drinking horns from the Sutton Hoo burial described under No. 053 (For information on this burial see 047) [4.64-66]

099 (right) – Zoomorphic ornament composed from facing pairs of fabulous animals, interlacing snake bodies and pear-shaped tail ends. Relief carved on the upper part of the wooden sword sheath from Nydam I, late 4th to early 5th c. (Denmark) [6.274-275, 13.286-287]

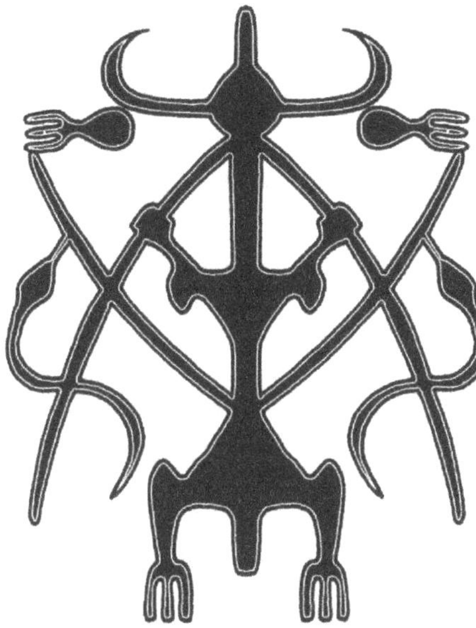

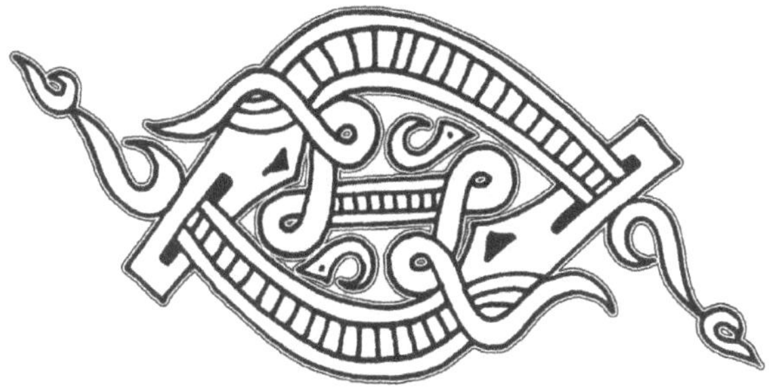

100 (left) – Carolingian animal figure on a fibula. Gotland, ca. 750-800 CE [11.Table 264, Fig. 2145; 10.76, Fig. 2145]

101 (right) – Late Animal Style II pattern on a gilded bronze belt buckle. Gotland, ca. 550-600 CE [11.Table 26, Fig. 276; 10.20, Fig. 276]

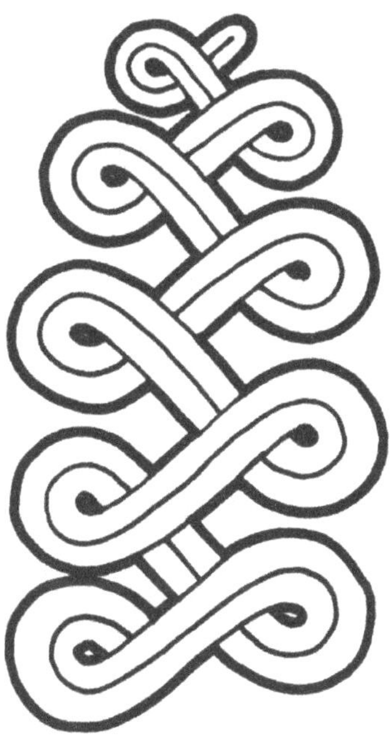

102 (left) – Plait ornament on the upper, inclined surface of the silver gilt pommel of the sword found in the Staffordshire Hoard (England), although it is probably a continental import (For the main theme from the head, see No. 186 and 125). 7th c. [9108, http://www.staffordshirehoard.org.uk/gallery/swords]

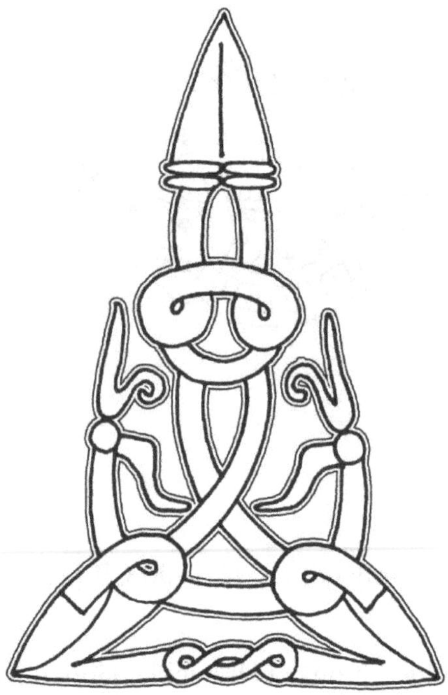

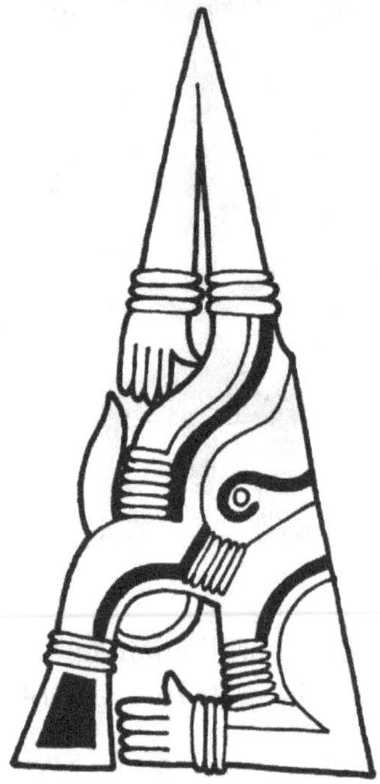

103 (left) – A motif from a drinking horn terminal from Taplow, Buckingamshire, is one of the very first representatives of Animal Style I in Anglo-Saxon England. It is an example of a riddling motif, which means that one can read its meaning in more than one way, depending on its horizontal or vertical position: as a crouching animal looking backwards, or as a stylized mask with a scrolled mouth. It is worth mentioning that such vessels were shared by the lord and his men and passed on in a circulating manner during feasts, which provided that he shared the care of the mythical forces he enjoyed. In return, he was granted the loyalty of the band, thence the symbolism of these decorations which appear to be different depending on the position of the horn. Early 6th century (another motif from this horn is described under No. 104) [17.31, 34, 57-58]

104 (right) – Style I motif called "helmet and hand" on the triangular plaques adorning the horn from Taplow (see above under No. 103) [17.31, 34, 57-58]

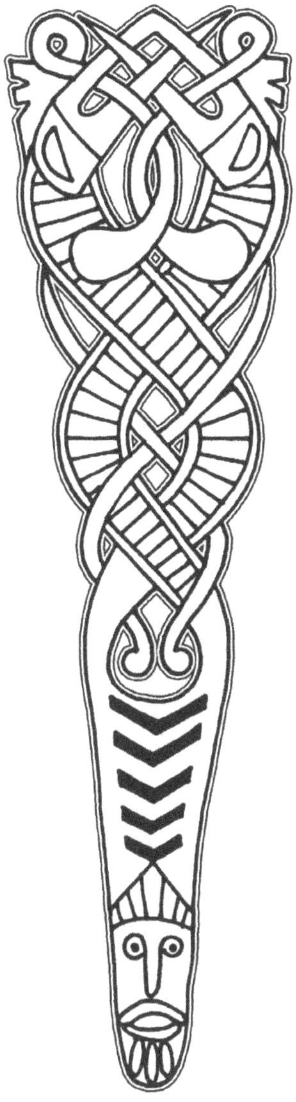

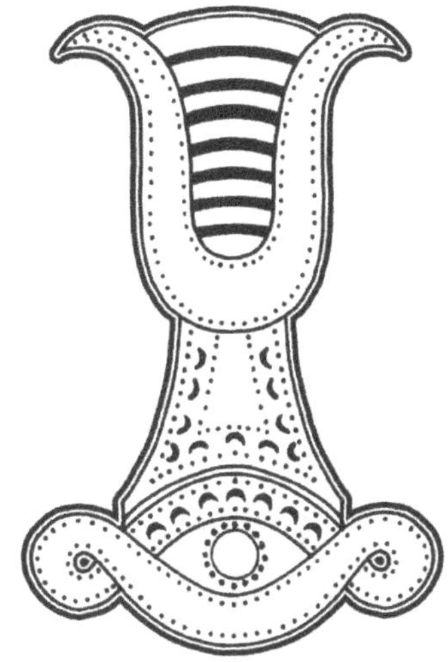

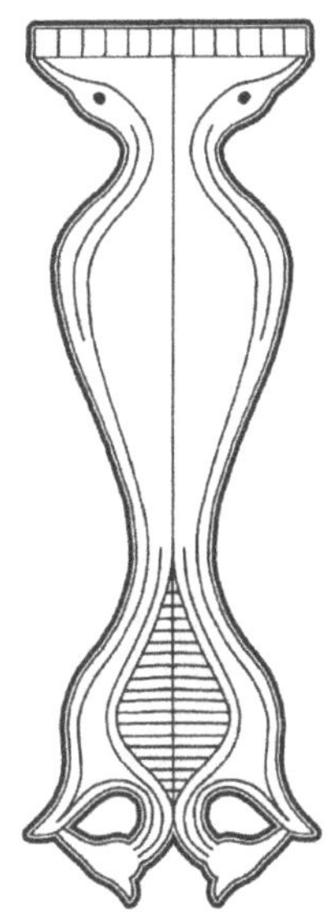

105 (left) – Zoomorphic ornament on gilded silver panels decorating maplewood bottles from the Sutton Hoo burial described under No. 053 (For information on this burial see 047) [4.64-66]

106 (top right) – Zoomorphic element of a harness in early Animal Style II. Gotland, ca. 550-600 CE [11.Table 76, Fig. 674; 10.31, Fig. 674]

107 (bottom right) – Zoomorphic ornament of fabulous animals with heads of beast on one end of the body, and that of a bird on the other. Relief carved on the upper part of the wooden sword sheath from Nydam I, late 4th to early 5th c. (Denmark) [13.286-287]

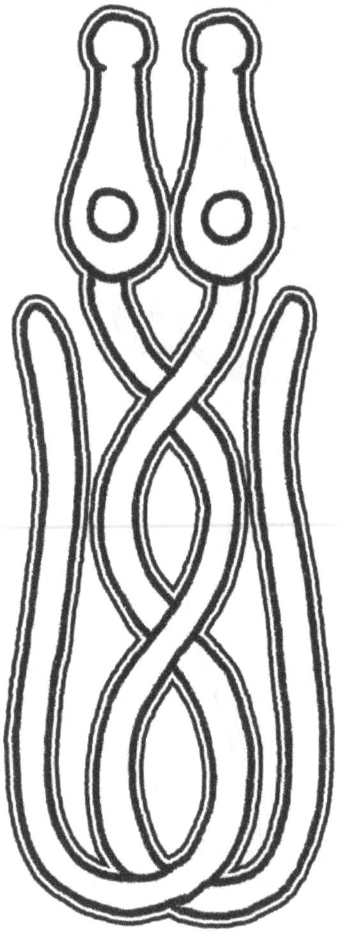

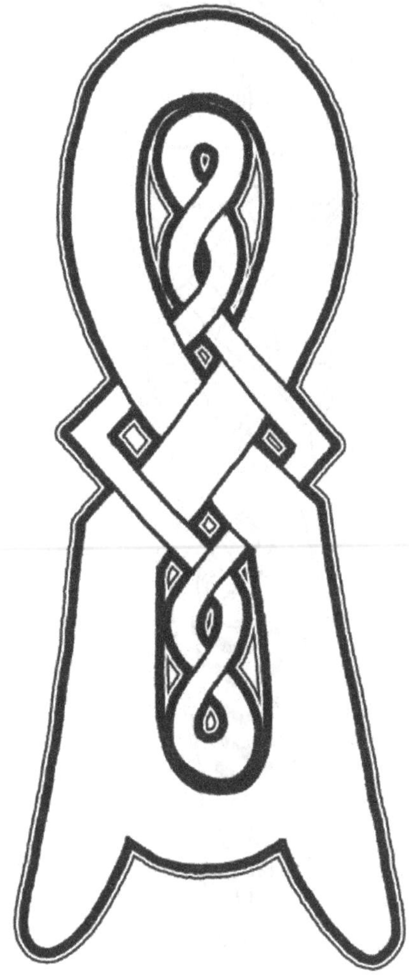

108 (left) – Decoration of the upper surface of the triangular upper guard of a ring-pommel Gotland, ca. 550-600 CE (For other details of this pommel see No. 110, 124, and 126) [11.Table 52, Fig. 521b; 10.27, Fig. 521]

109 (right) – Bronze decorations on a helmet. Gotland, ca. 550-600 CE [11.Table. 69, Fig. 617; 10.30, Fig. 617]

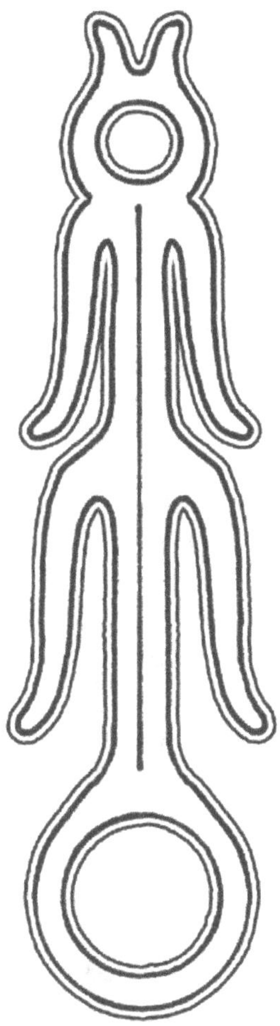

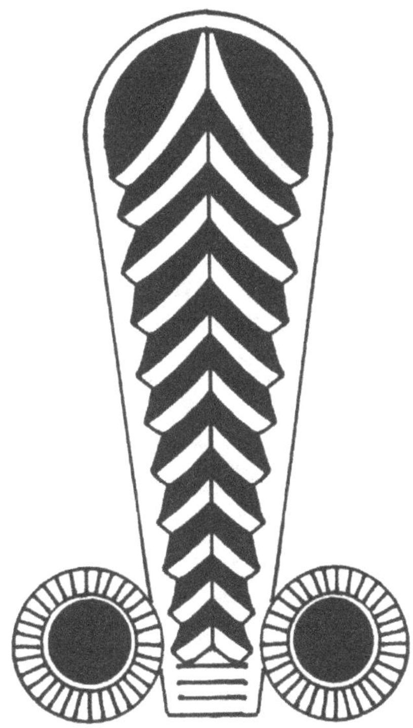

110 (left) – Ornament from the other side of No. 108 [11.Table 52, Fig. 521b; 10.27, Fig. 521]

111 (right) – Ornament on an animal head buckle. Gotland, ca. 550-600 CE [11.Table. 26, Fig. 280; 10.20-21, Fig. 280]

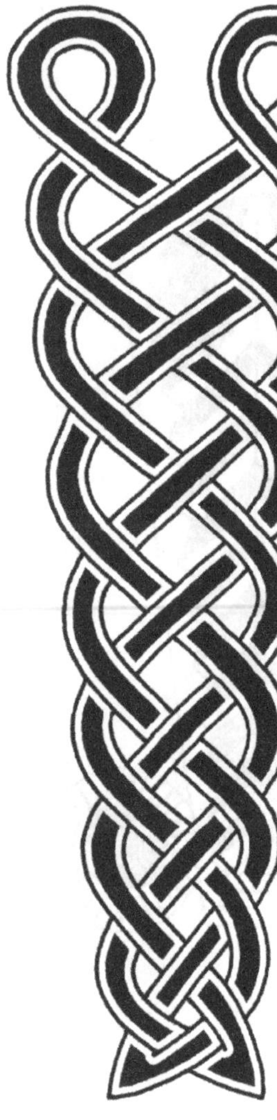

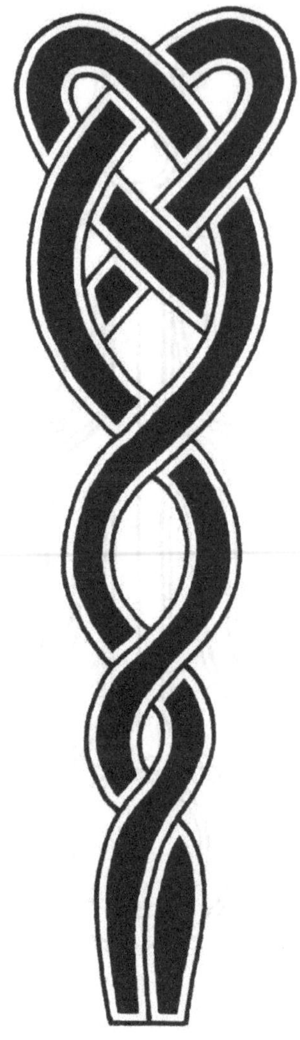

112 (left) – Plait pattern on a bronze overlay on the iron fitting on a shield. Gotland, ca. 550-600 CE [11.Table 75, Fig. 659; 10.31, Fig. 659]

113 (right) – Plait pattern from a gilded bronze element of a harness shaped like an animal head in Style II. Gotland, ca. 550-600 CE [11.Table 77, Fig. 676; 10.32, Fig. 676]

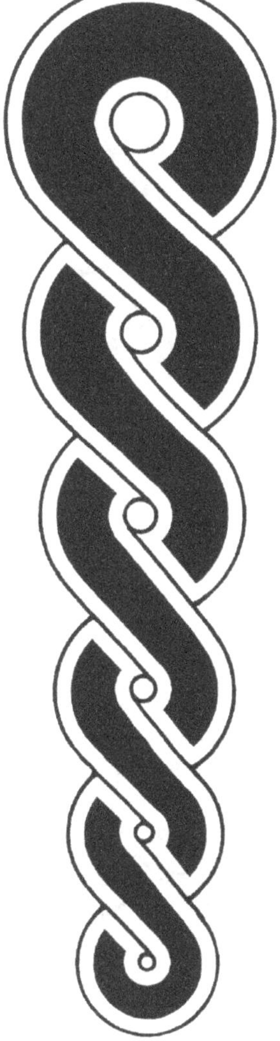

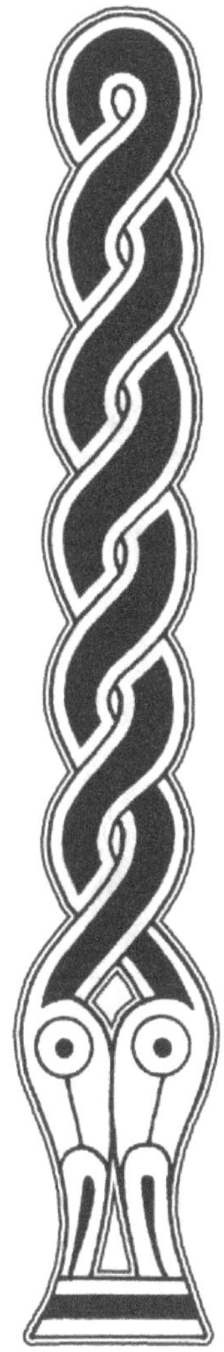

114 (left) – Plait ornament from a fibula. Gotland, ca. 550-600 CE (Also see No. 147) [11.Table. 7, Fig. 53; 10.13, Fig. 53]

115 (right) – Zoomorphic ornament in early Animal Style II from the belt strap end from a man's burial. Gotland, ca. 550-600 CE. (Also see No. 078) [11.Table 24, Fig. 266; 10.20, Fig. 266]

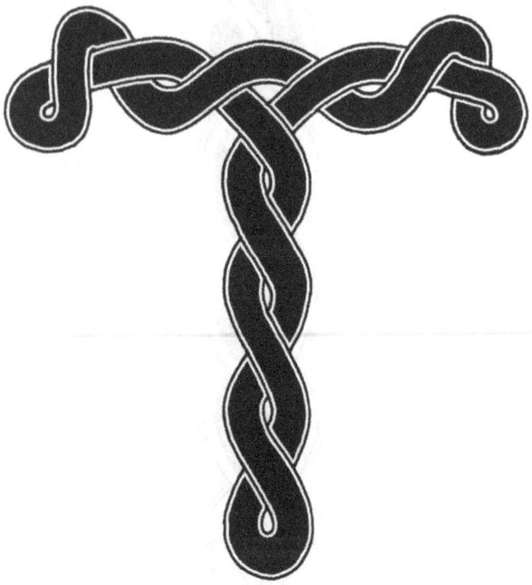

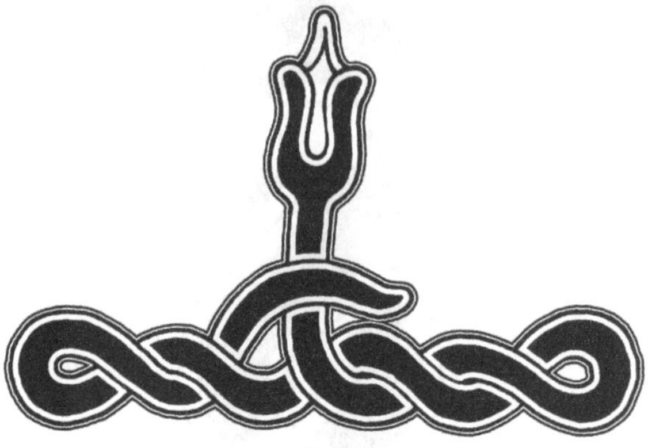

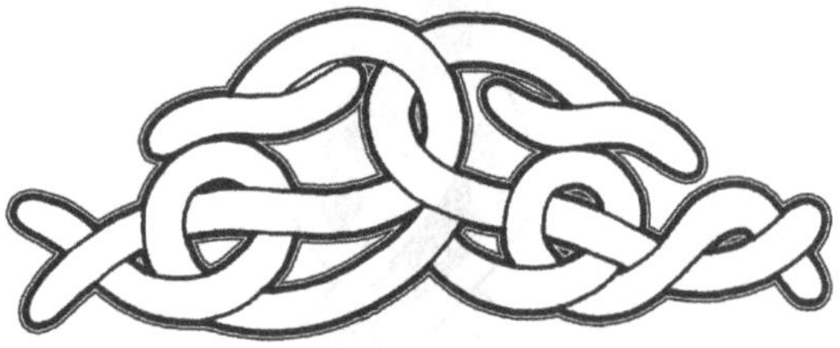

116 (left) – Plait ornament from a fibula. Gotland, ca. 550-600 CE [11.Table. 7, Fig. 59; 10.13, Fig. 59]

117 (top right) – Plait filigree motif on the Sutton Hoo fibula described under No. 060 (for the burial see No. 047) [1. plate I]

118 (bottom right) – Ornament on a gold upper guard of the sword from Lincolnshire (England), 7th c. [9.31]

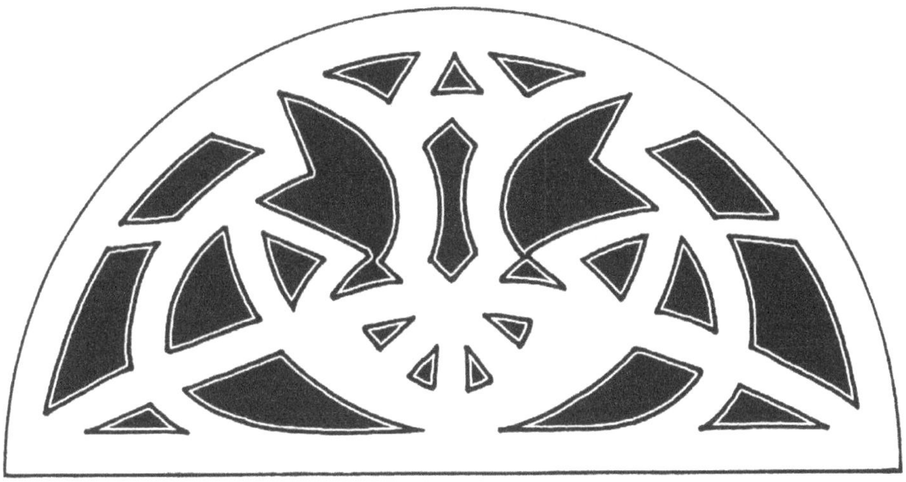

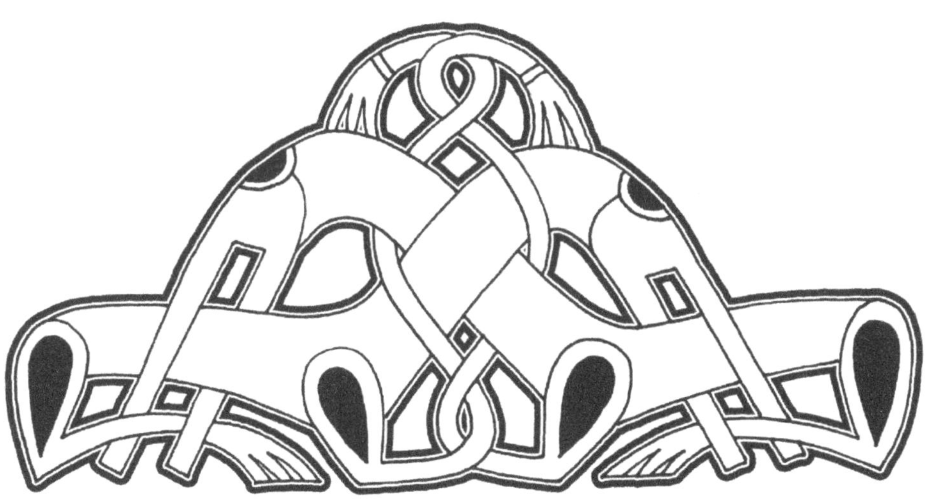

119 (top) – One of the zoomorphic ornaments on the boss of the shield from the Vendel XI burial (For information on this site see No. 059, for another element of this boss see No. 093) [9.128]

120 (bottom) – Zoomorphic pattern in Style II on a silver gilded pommel of the sword from a Crudale Down burial, Kent (England), 7th c. [17.67]

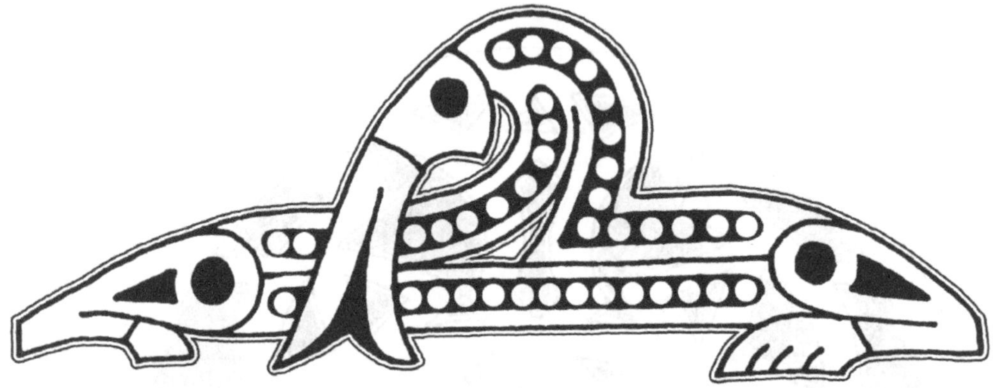

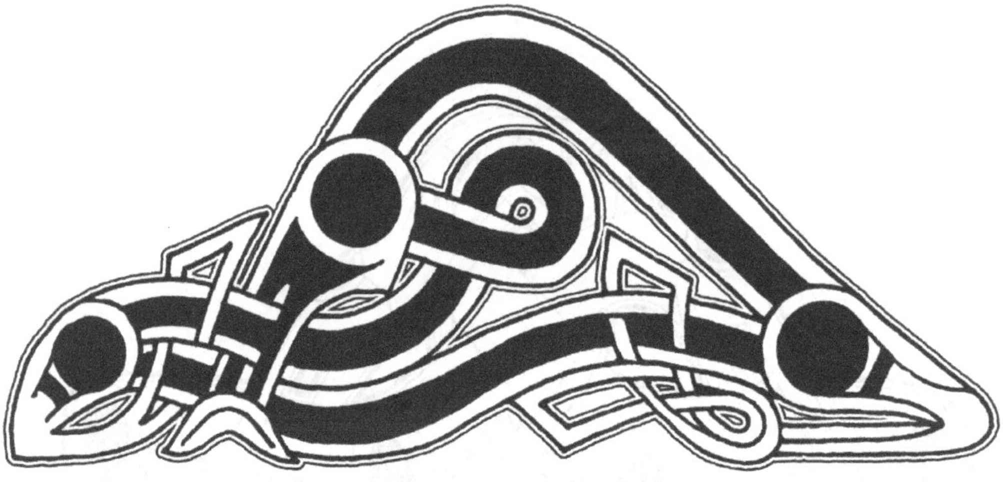

121 (top) – Late Animal Style II ornament on a bronze, partly silvered triangular upper sword guard. Gotland, ca. 650-700 CE [11.Table 200, Fig. 1668; 10.60, Fig. 1668]

122 (bottom) – As above (ornament from the other side of No. 129) [11.Table 200, Fig. 1669; 10.60, Fig. 1669]

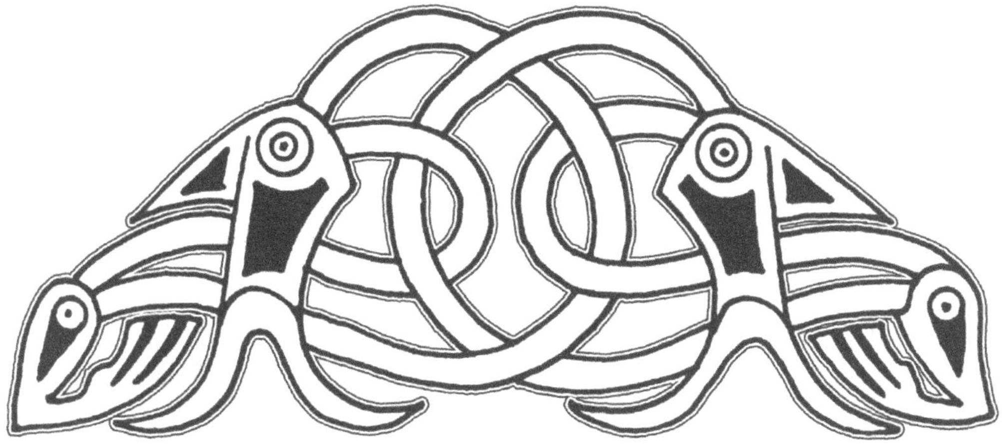

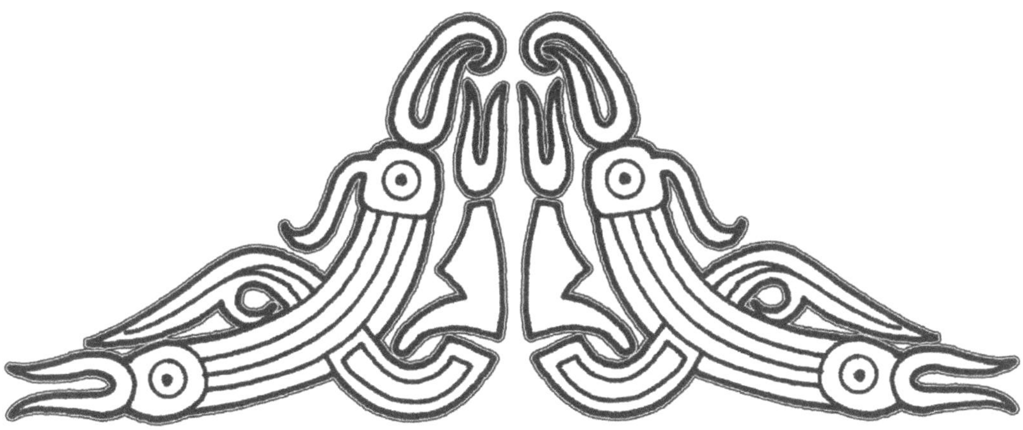

123 (top) – As above, early Animal Style II. Gotland, ca. 550-600 CE (Also see No. 138) [11.Table. 54, Fig. 525a; 10.27, Fig. 525]

124 (bottom) – Early Animal Style II ornament on the flat part of the guard of a sword described under No. 108. Gotland, ca. 550-600 CE [11.Table 52, Fig. 521a; 10.27, Fig. 521]

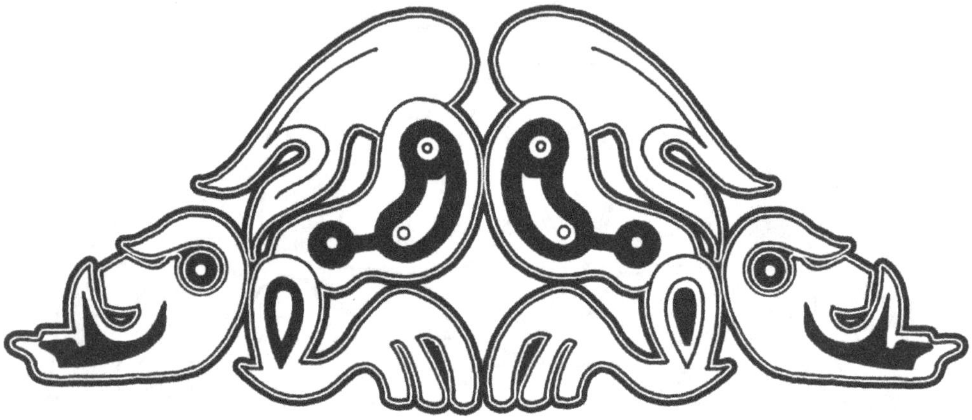

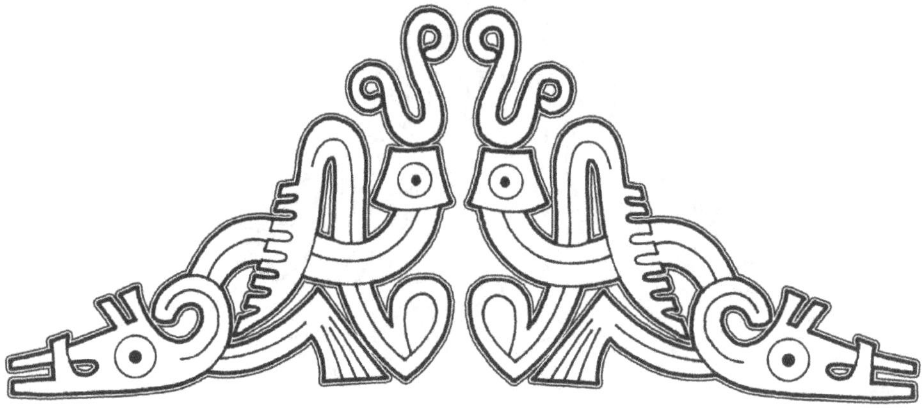

125 (top) – Zoomorphic pattern showing boar heads, pommel of the Staffordshire sword (See No. 102 and 186) [9.108; http://www.staffordshirehoard.org.uk/gallery/swords]

126 (bottom) – Early Animal Style II ornament on the flat part of the guard of a sword described under No. 108. Gotland, ca. 550-600 CE [11.Table 52, Fig. 521b; 10.27, Fig. 521]

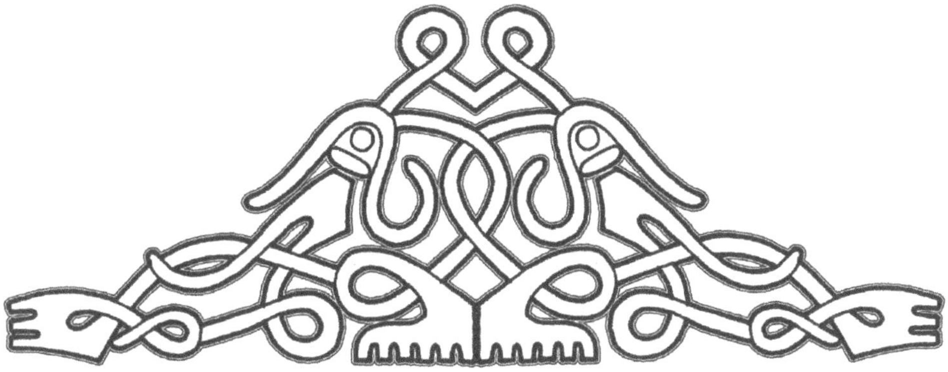

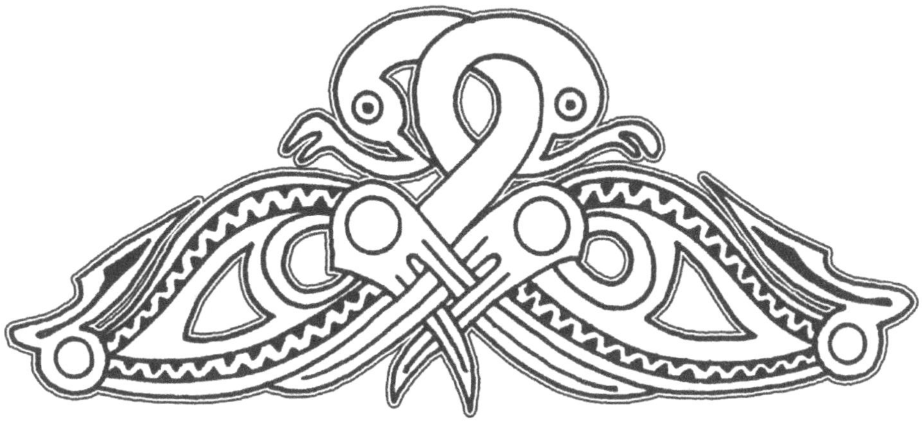

127 (top) – Early Animal Style II ornament on a upper guard of a sword. Gotland, ca. 550-600 CE [11.Table 52, Fig. 520; 10.27, Fig. 520]

128 (bottom) – Animal Style II ornament on a bronze upper sword guard. Gotland, ca. 600-650 CE [11.Table 133, Fig. 1181a; 10.45, Fig. 1181]

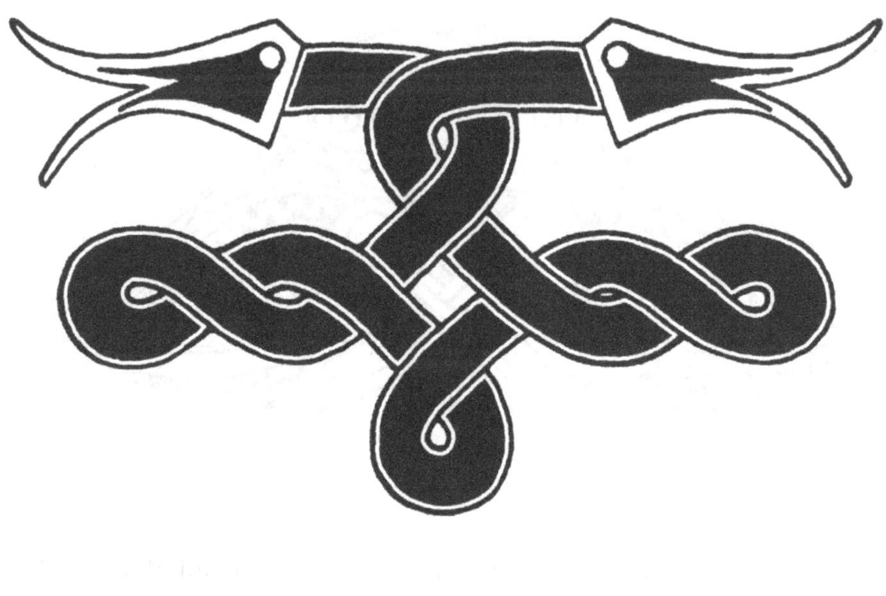

129 (top) – See No. 122

130 (bottom) – Another ornament from the fibula described under No. 116

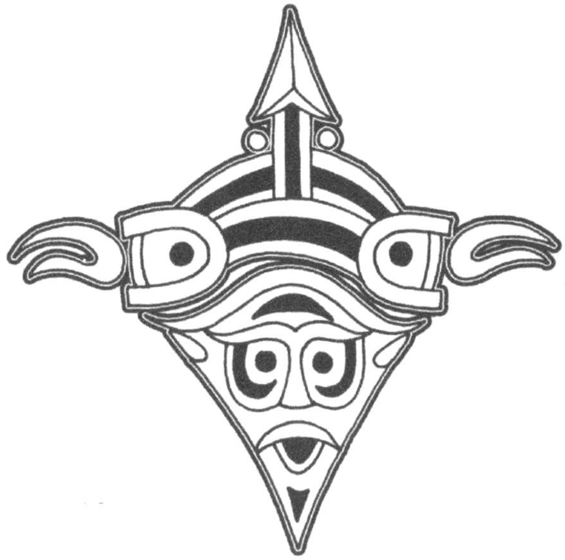

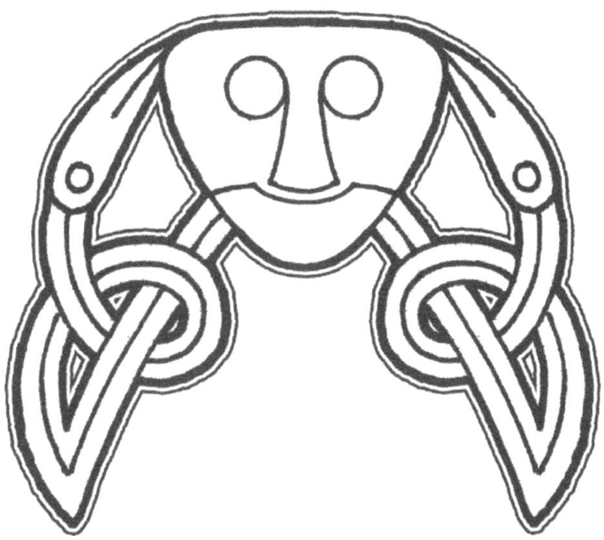

131 (top) – Bearded human mask wearing a helmet or cap, adorned with two birds' heads and a central motif on the foot-plate of a brooch from Chessell Down. (See No. 026), perhaps what we have here is the image of a horned man, early 6th c. [17.16]

132 (bottom) – Human head and Style II zoomorphic figures on the frame of a buckle. Gotland, ca. 650-700 CE [11.Table 172, Fig. 1440; 10.54, Fig. 1440]

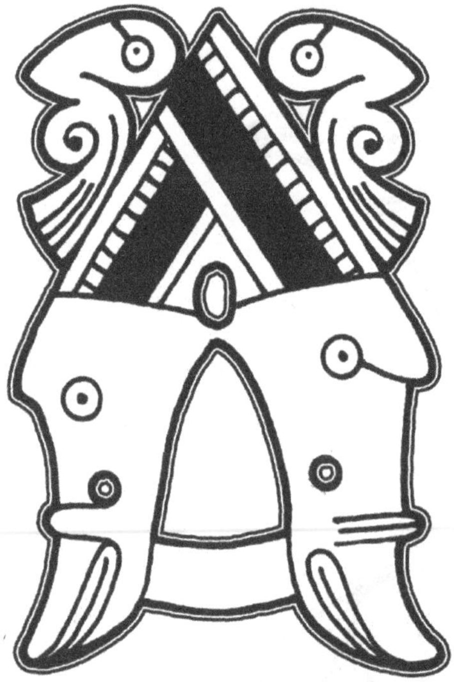

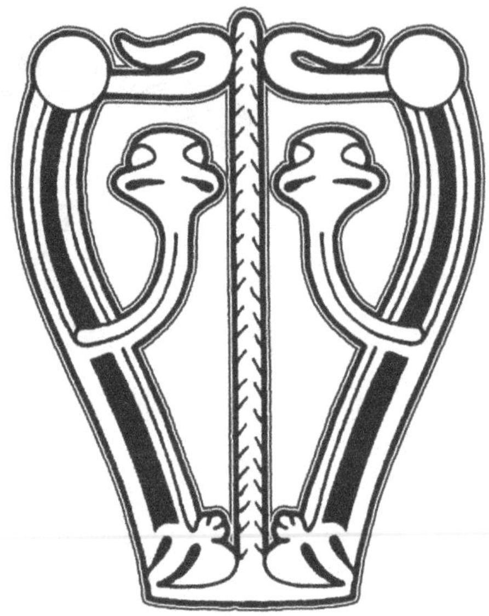

133 (top) – Bronze belt attachment with two boar heads. Gotland, ca. 550-600 CE [11. Table. 35, Fig. 378; 10.23, Fig. 378]

134 (bottom) – Two Animal Style III serpents on a fibula. Gotland, ca. 750-800 CE [11. Table 264, Fig. 2143; 10.76, Fig. 2143]

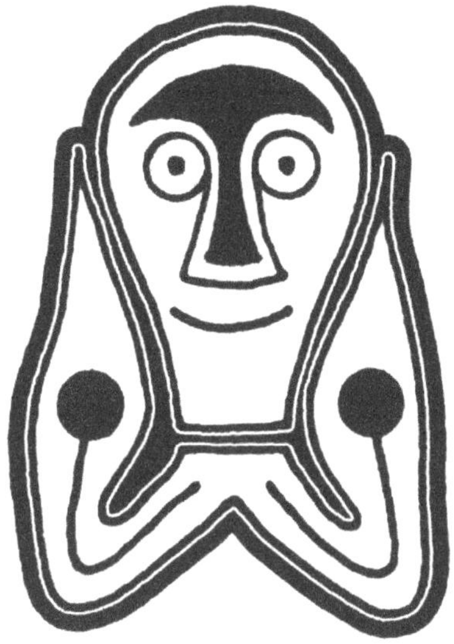

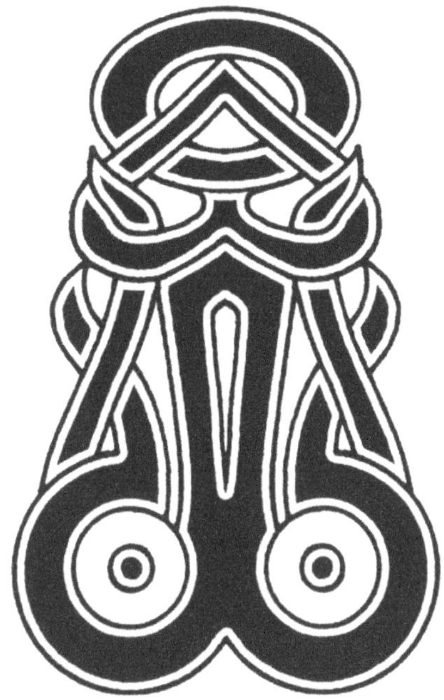

135 (top) – Zoomorphic bronze fittings on a shield boss (Also see 066). Gotland, ca. 600-650 CE [11.Table 142, Fig. 1239; 10.47, Fig. 1239]

136 (bottom) – Human figure on the upper rim of the upper guard of the sword described under 128 [11.Table 133, Fig. 1181b; 10.45, Fig. 1181]

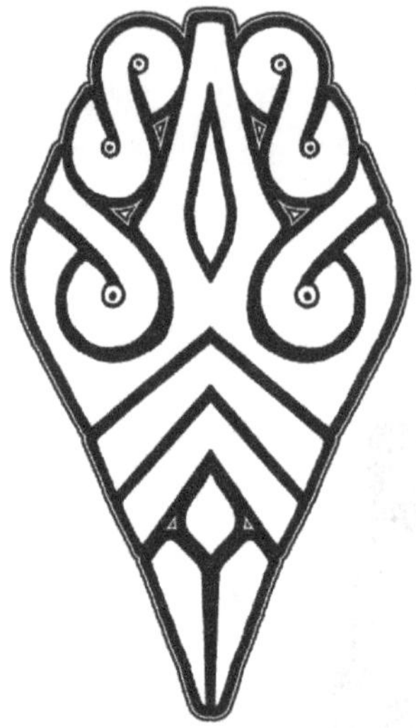

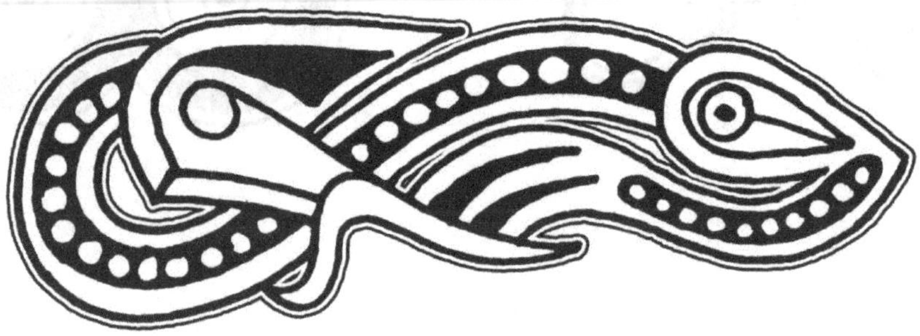

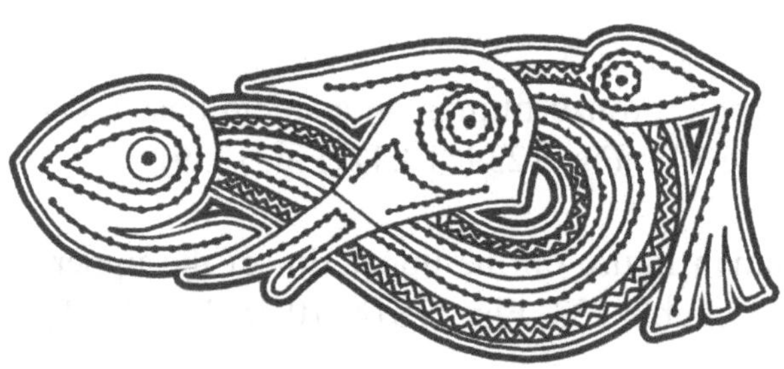

137 (top) – Motif on the foot plate of a gilded, silver Ostrogoth bow fibula from the time of Theoderic the Great, 5th-6th c., Reggio Emilia, Italy (Also see 29) [12, dwg. 22]

138 (middle) – Decoration of the upper surface of the sword guard described under No. 123

139 (bottom) – Animal Style II ornament from a harness. Gotland, ca. 550-600 CE [11. Table 76, Fig. 672; 10.31, Fig. 672]

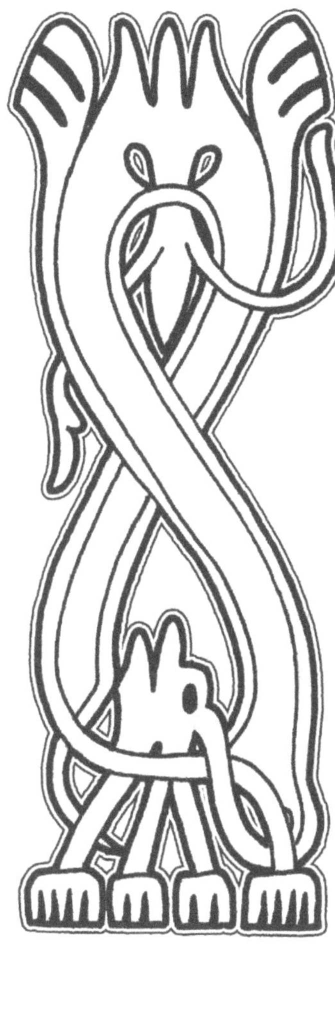

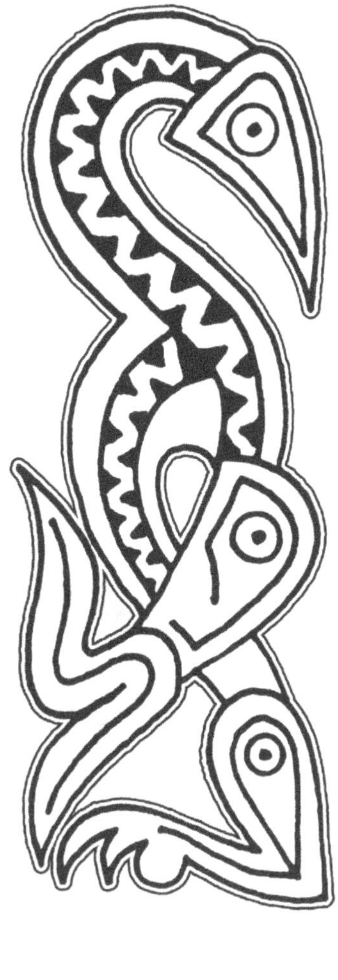

140 (left) – Zoomorphic ornament on the rim of a round fibula. Gotland, ca. 700-750 CE [11.Table 221, Fig. 1814; 10.65, Fig. 1814]

141 (right) – Zoomorphic ornament from the swords described under No. 128 and 136 [11.Table 133, Fig. 1181b; 10.45, Fig. 1181]

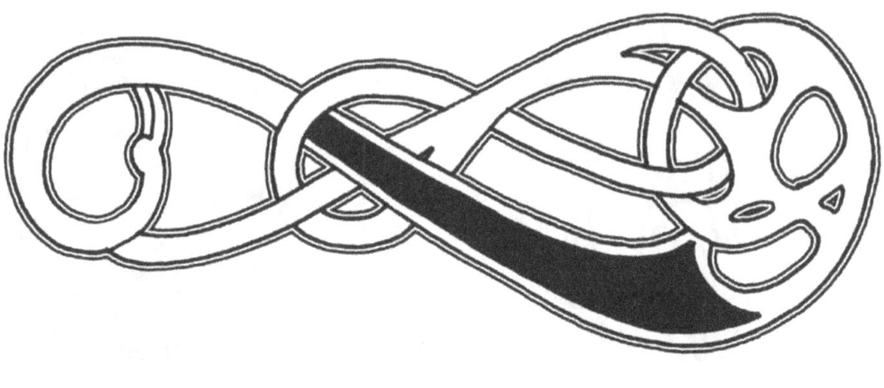

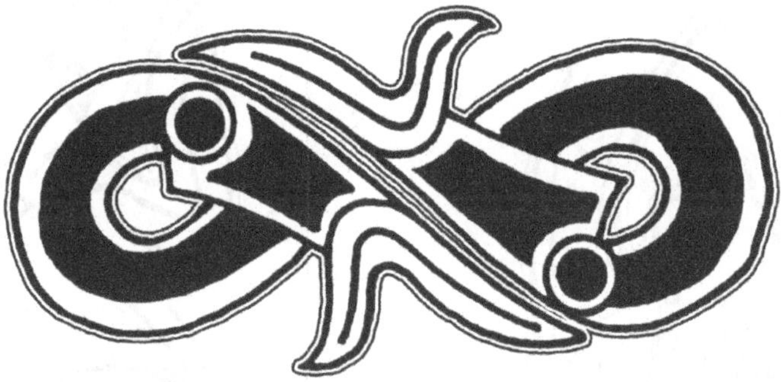

142 (top) – Cut work panel of an animal in Style II. Gotland, ca. 750-800 CE [11. Table 290, Fig. 2306; 10.80, Fig. 2306]

143 (bottom) – Early Animal Style II ornament on a rectangular belt strap plate. Gotland, ca. 550-600 CE [11.Table 29, Fig. 316; 10.21, Fig. 316]

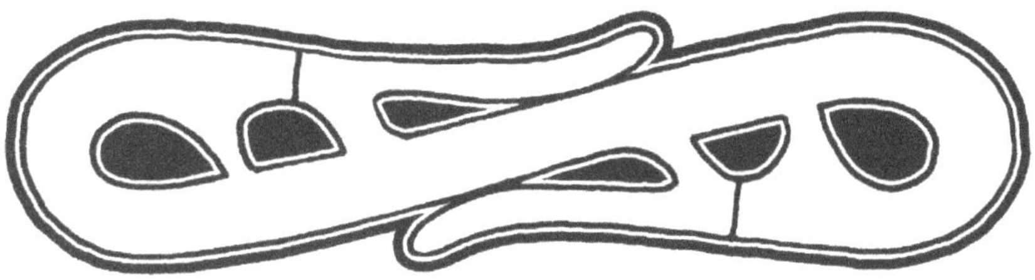

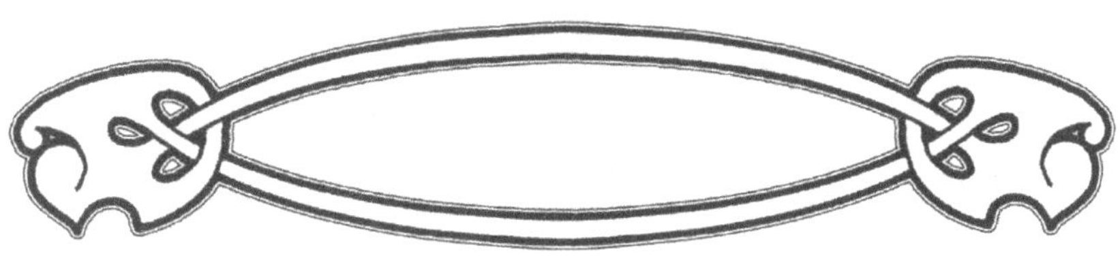

144 (top) – Iron cut-work S-shaped belt attachment in later Animal Style. Gotland, ca. 650-700 CE [11.Table 190, Fig. 1579; 10.58, Fig. 1579]

145 (bottom) – Oval plate with zoomorphic figures in Style III. Gotland, ca. 700-750 CE [11.Table 239, Fig. 1970; 10.69, Fig. 1970]

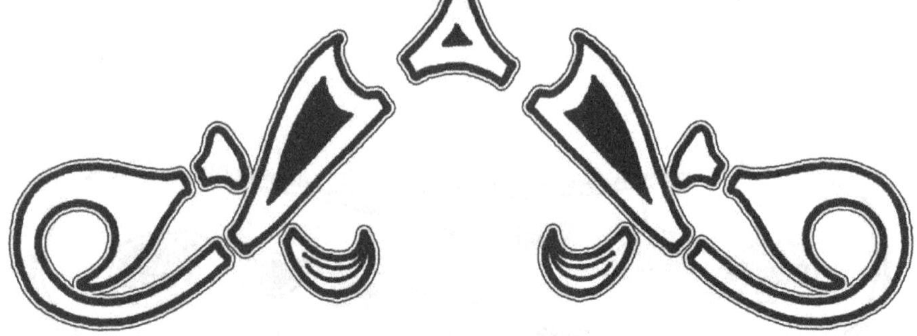

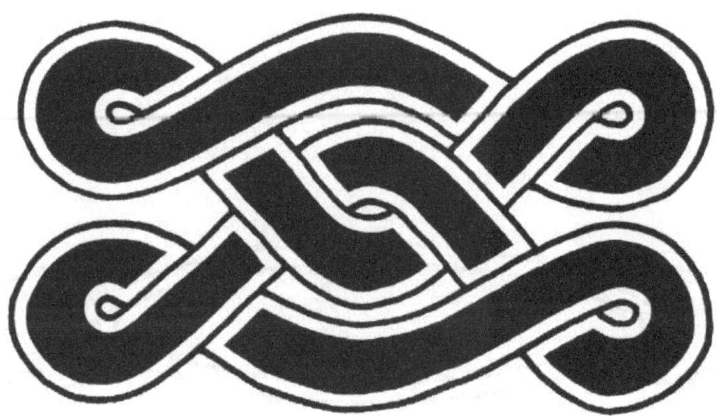

146 (top) – Decoration on the side of a bronze pommel of a sword. Gotland, ca. 700-750 CE. The custom of decorating the rounded surfaces of sword guards was not previously known in Gotland and is a continental borrowing (For ornaments on the other side, see 171, 172) [11.Table 250, Fig. 2050b; 10.72, Fig. 2050]

147 (bottom) – See 114

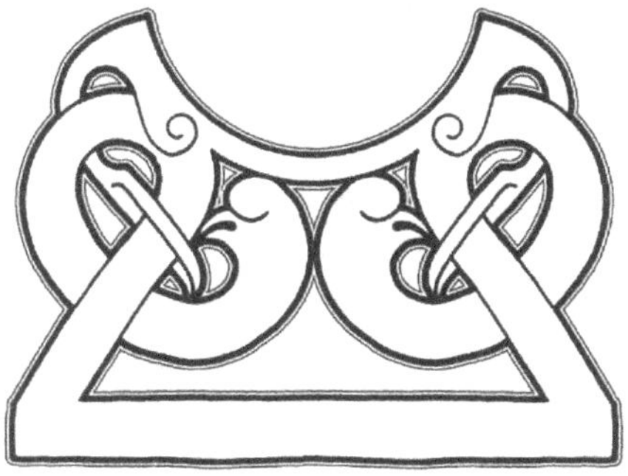

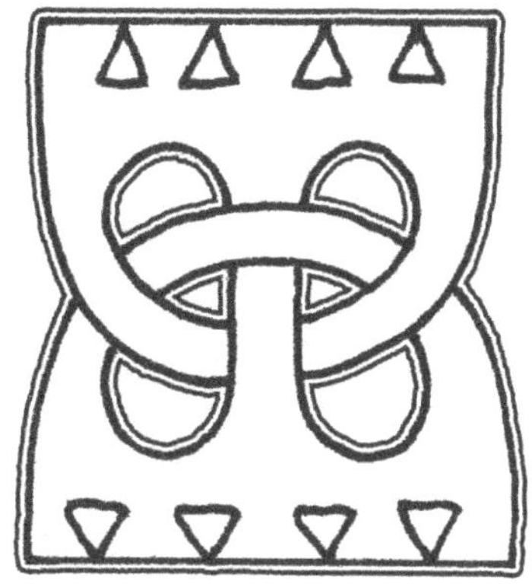

148 (left) – Two Animal Style III figures on the frame of a buckle. Gotland, ca. 700-750 CE [11.Table 227, Fig. 1870; 10.67, Fig. 1870]

149 (right) – Ornament on the rim of a fibula described under No. 034 (Also see No. 238)

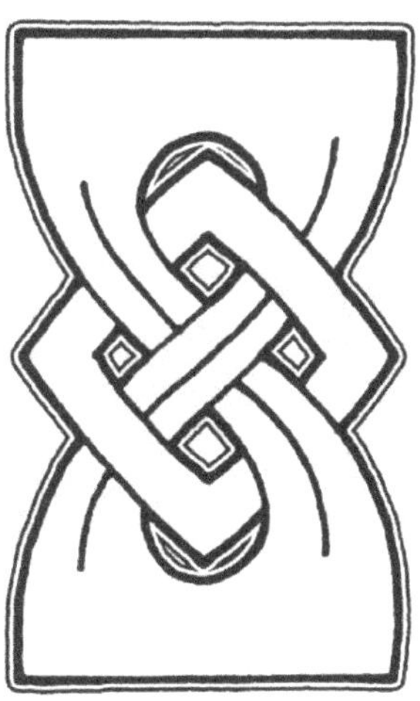

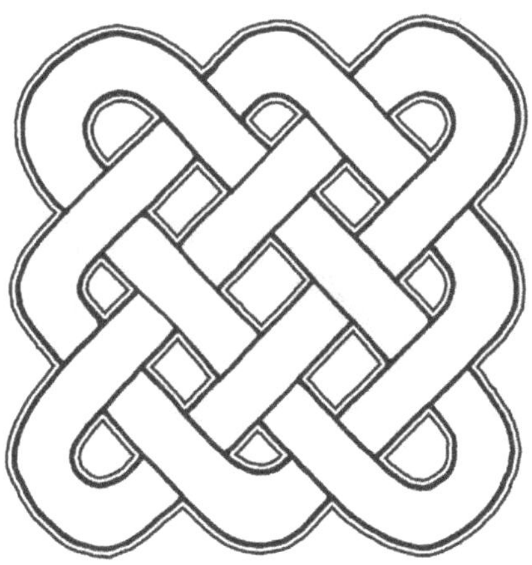

150 (left) – Small ornament on the rim of a round fibula (for the whole decoration of the upper surface of the fibula see No. 237). Roes, Gotland, ca. 700-750 CE [11 Table 224, Fig. 1833; 10.65, Fig. 1833]

151 (right) – Plait ornament on the bone paneling of a knife handle. Gotland, ca. 600-650 CE, [11.Table. 132, Fig. 1180; 10.45, Fig. 1180]

 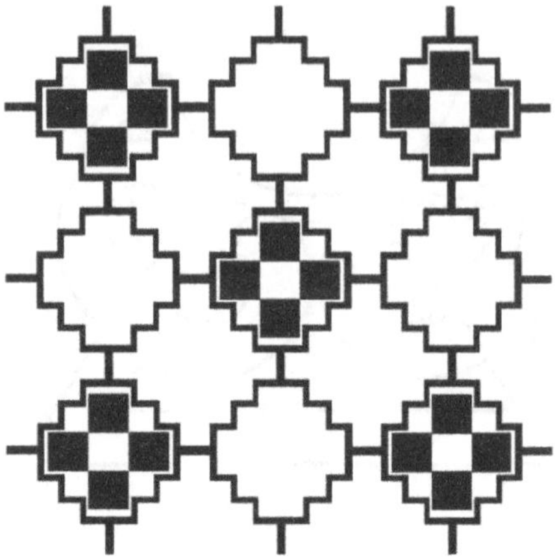

152 (left) – Ornament on the guard of a sword from Altlussheim/Mannheim (Germany), mid-5th c. [3. dwg. 35]

153 (right) – Enameled (cloisonné) ornament decorating the main panel of the clasps from Sutton Hoo described under No. 060 [4.87 and Plate VI; 1.Plate 1, 17.62]

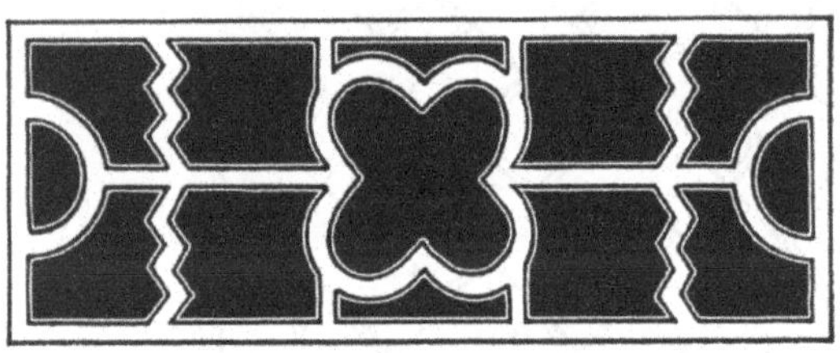 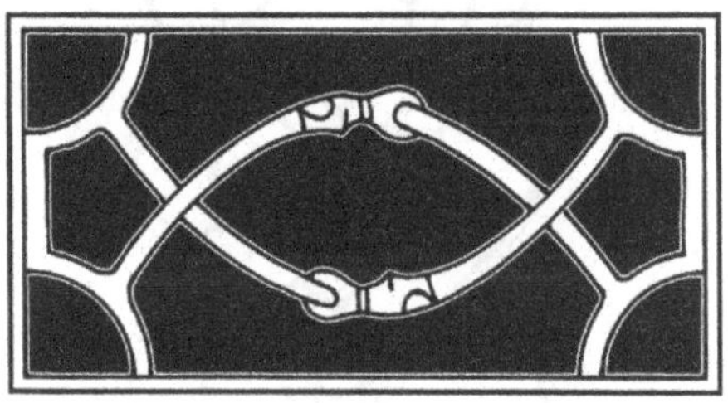

154 (left) – One of the cloisonné patterns form a gilded, silver fibula also in Germanic-Pontic Animal Style, from the Alemannic princess' grave from the Merovingian period. Wittislingen (Germany), ca. 600-650 CE (Also see No. 258) [3.84]

155 (right) – Early Animal Style III ornament on a rectangular belt strap plate. Gotland, ca. 700-750 CE [11.Table 241, Fig. 1981; 10.70, Fig. 1981]

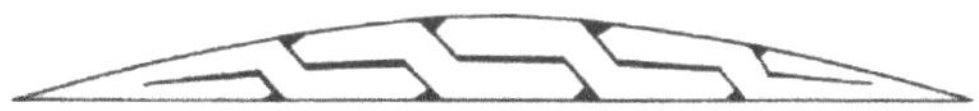

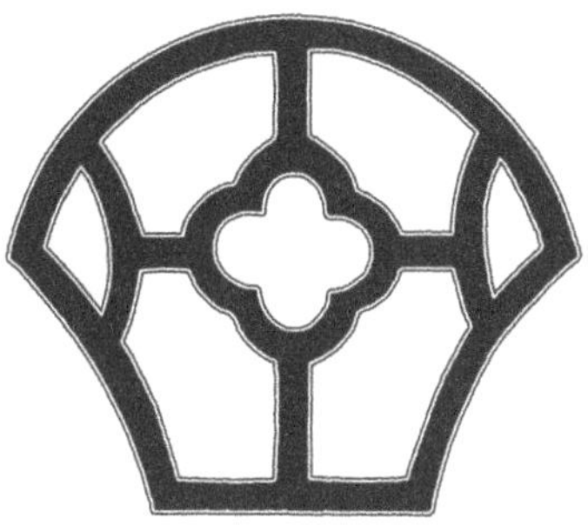

156 (left) – Simple ornament on the main element of an antler comb. Gotland, ca. 700-750 CE [11.Table. 241, Fig. 1993; 10.70, Fig. 1993]

157 (right) – Chape of the buckle described under No. 003, with carbuncles.

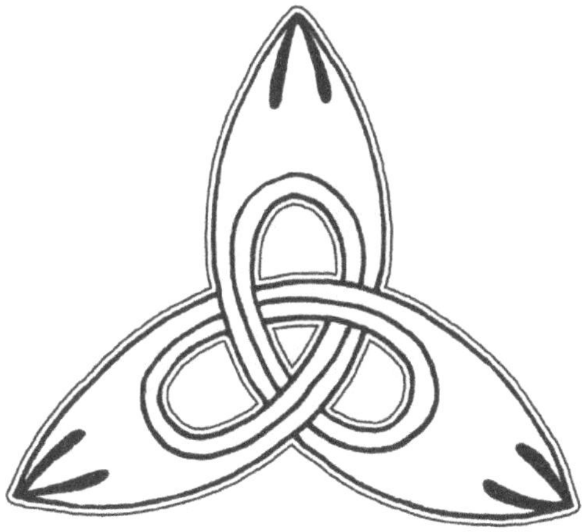

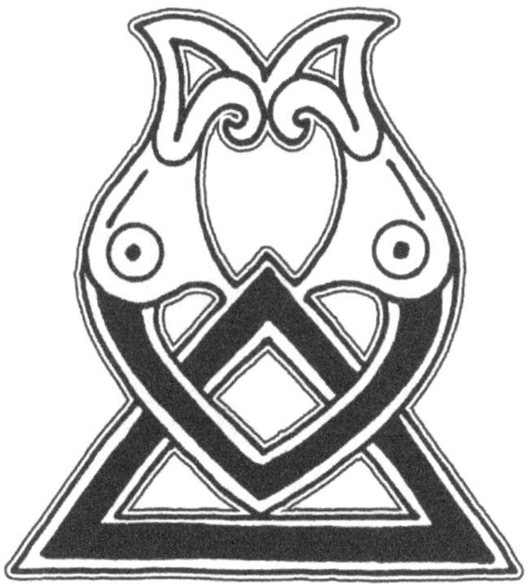

158 (left) – Small detail from the corners of the ornament on the lower part of a large fibula. This ornament became common later, in the Viking Age. Gotland, ca. 750-800 CE [11.Table 266, Fig. 2152; 10.76-77, Fig. 2152]

159 (right) – Animal heads in Style II as an inner ornament on a cut-work U-shaped belt attachment. Gotland, ca. 600-650 CE [11.Table 119, Fig. 1054; 10.42, Fig. 1054]

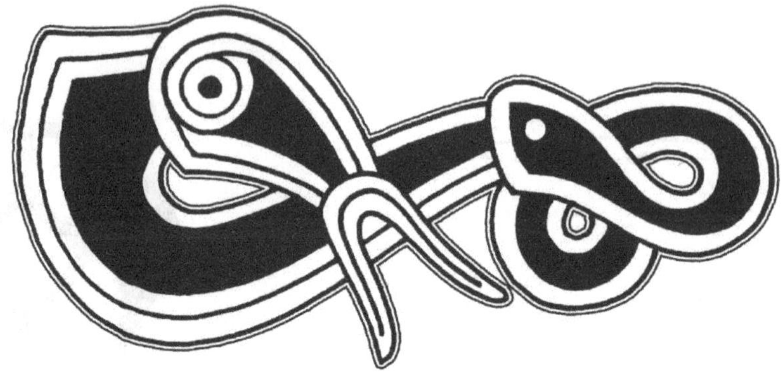

160 – Animal Style II ornament on a belt strap end plate. Gotland, ca. 550-600 CE [11.Table 21, Fig. 229; 10.19, Fig. 229]

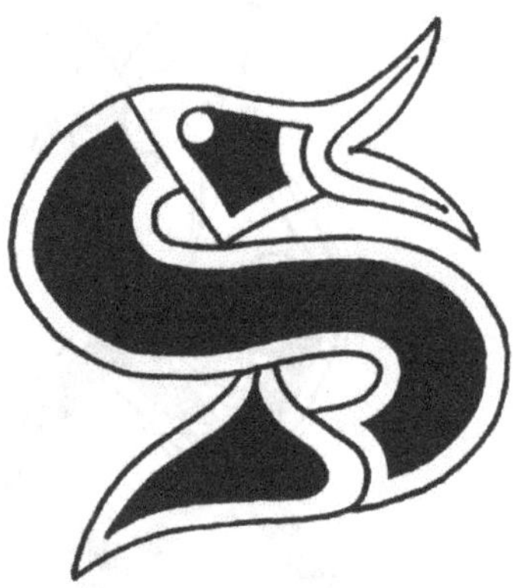

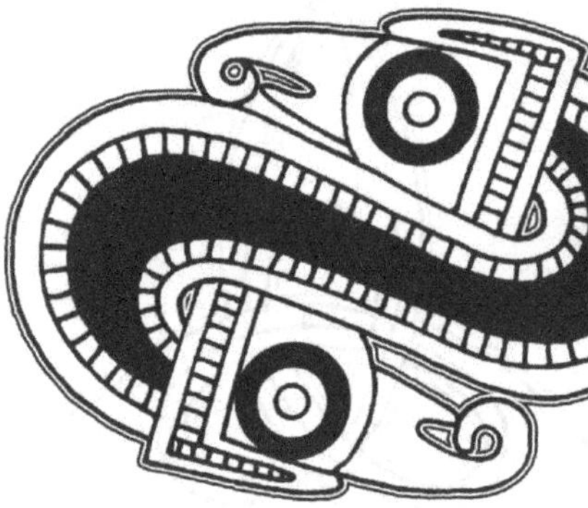

161 (left) – Early Animal Style II ornament on a square element of a harness. Gotland, ca. 550-600 CE [11.Table 81, Fig. 698; 10.32, Fig. 698]

162 (right) – S-shaped fibula with bird-of-prey head terminals. Gotland, ca. 550-600 CE [11.Table 13, Fig. 103; 10.15, Fig. 103]

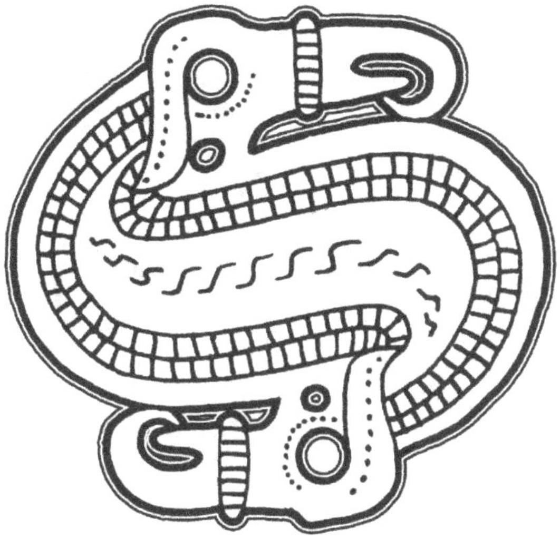

163 – As above [11.Table 13, Fig. 104; 10.15, Fig. 104]

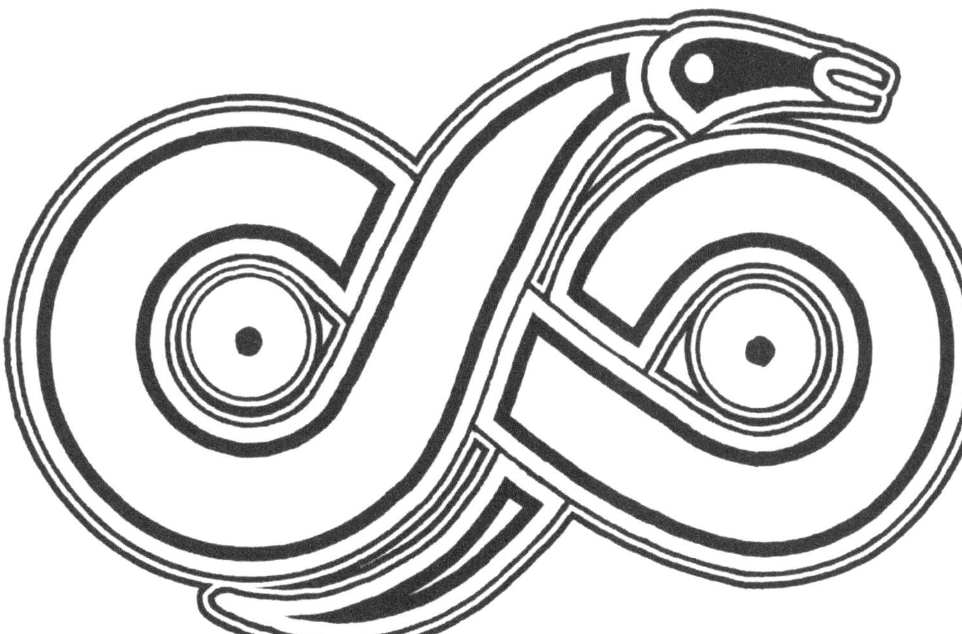

164 – Curled serpent-shaped fibula. Gotland, ca. 550-600 CE [11.Table. 13, Fig. 107; 10.15, Fig. 107]

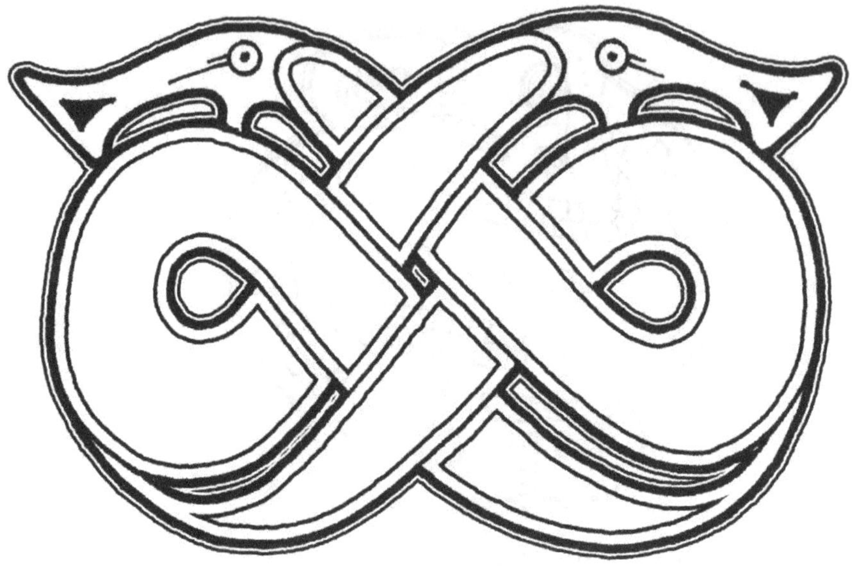

165 – Fibula, in the shape of two interlacing serpents. Visible development of earlier single fibulae (See above, No. 164) Gotland, ca. 600-650 CE [11. Table 108, Fig. 915; 10.38, Fig. 915]

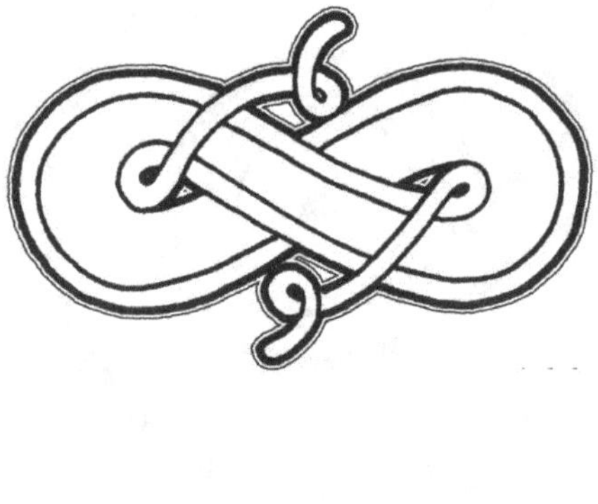

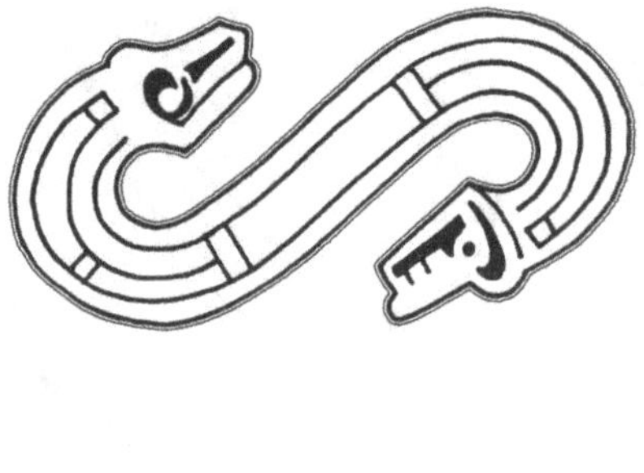

166 (left) – Ornament from a T-shaped, gilded bronze belt attachment. Gotland, ca. 550-600 CE [11. Table 35, Fig. 374; 10.23, Fig. 374]

167 (right) – S-shaped bronze belt attachment decorated with animal heads. Gotland, ca. 550-600 CE [11. Table 35, Fig. 376; 10.23, Fig. 376]

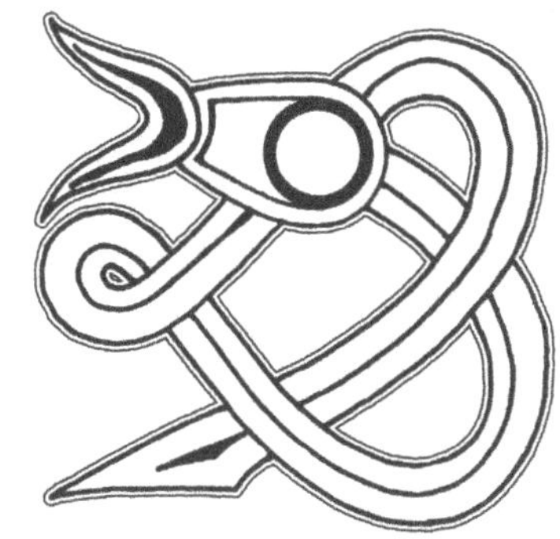

168 – as in No. 161 [11.Table 81, Fig. 697; 10.32, Fig. 697]

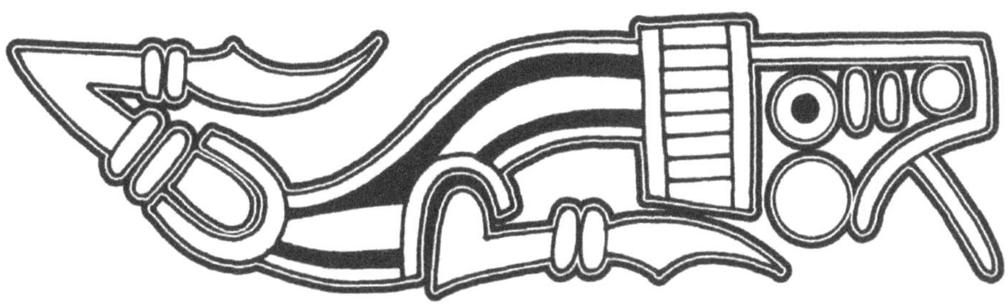

169 – Animal Style I detail of a fibula found in grave 41 at Bifrons, Kent (England), 5th-6th c. The style derives from one known from the bog deposits from Nydam, Denmark [17.55-56, Fig. 30]

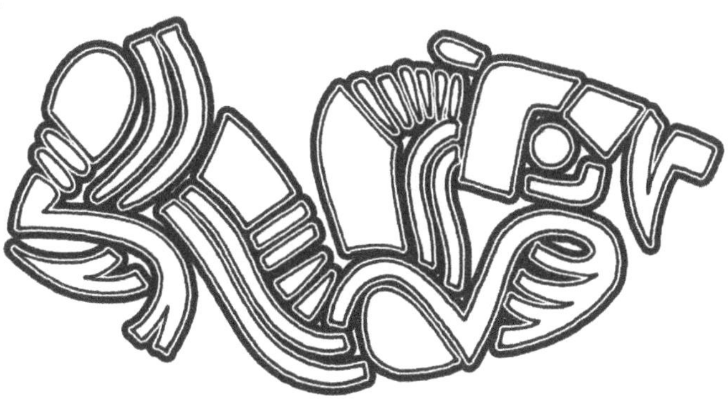

170 – Animal Style I detail from a fibula found in grave 63 at Bifrons, Kent (England), 5th-6th c. [17.55-56, Fig. 30]

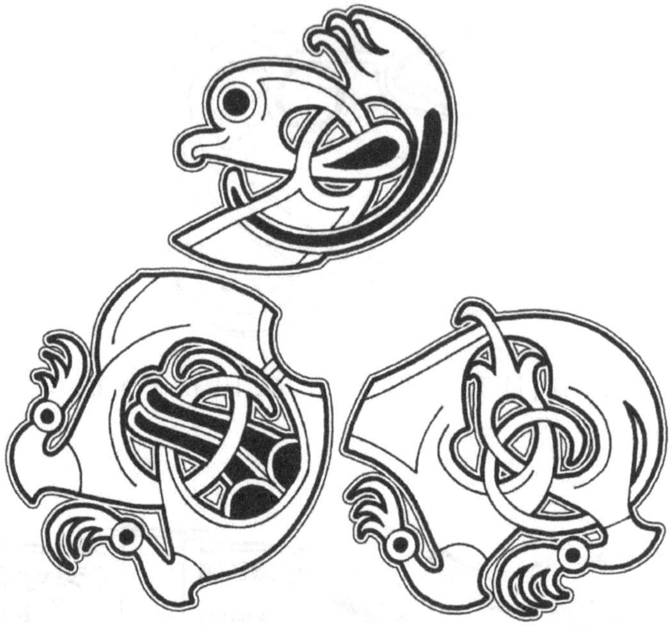

171 – Ornament on the other side of the pommel of the sword described under No. 146, showing four legged animals with bird heads, coming from the North-Eastern part of the Frankish area and mixed with Nordic Style III [11.Table 250, Fig. 2050e; 10.72, Fig. 2050]

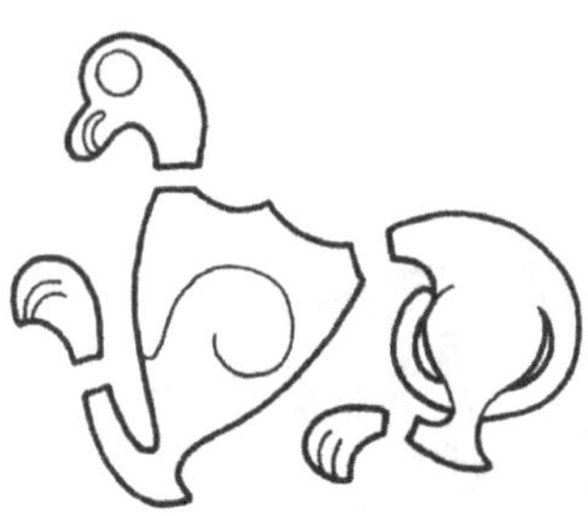

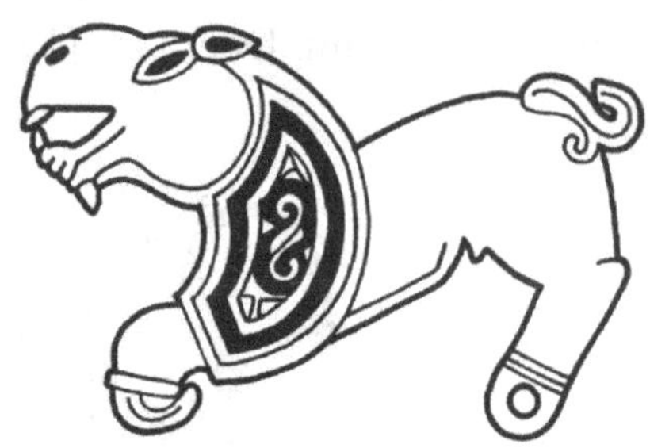

172 (left) – As above. [11.Table 250, Fig. 2050f; 10.72, Fig. 2050]

173 (right) – Silver plaque with an animal application (probably a hippopotamus, representing chthonic powers) from the Martynivka treasure (See No. 096) [British Museum; 16]

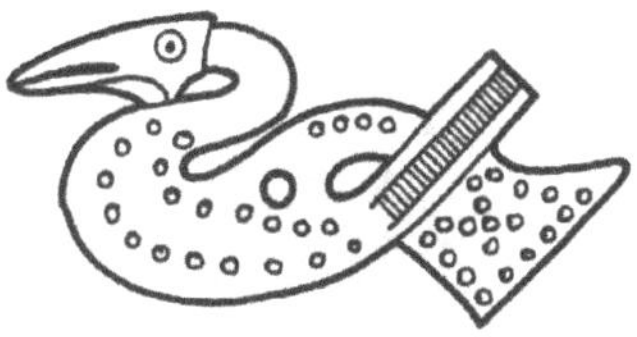

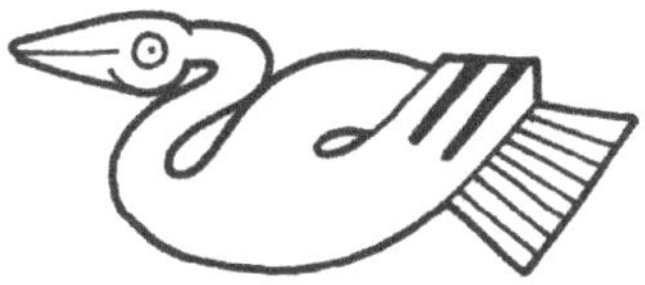

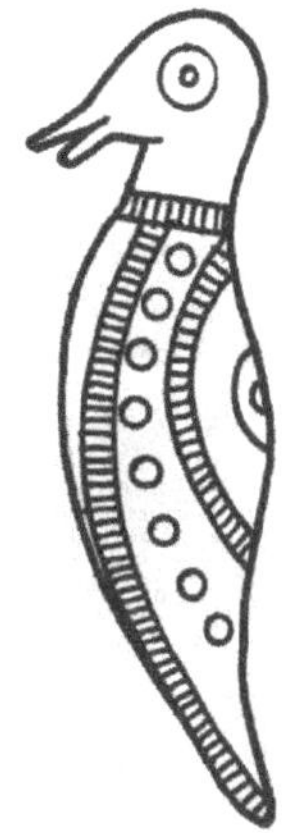

174 (left) – Small bird-shaped belt attachment (Also see No. 175, 176, 178) Gotland, ca. 550-600 CE, [11.Table 19, Fig. 204; 10.18, Fig. 204]

175 (center) – As above. [11.Table 19, Fig. 203; 10.18, Fig. 203]

176 (right) – As above. [11.Table 19, Fig. 199; 10.17, Fig. 199]

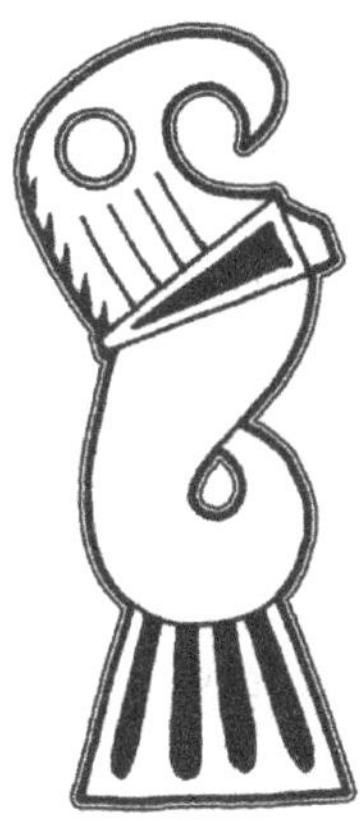

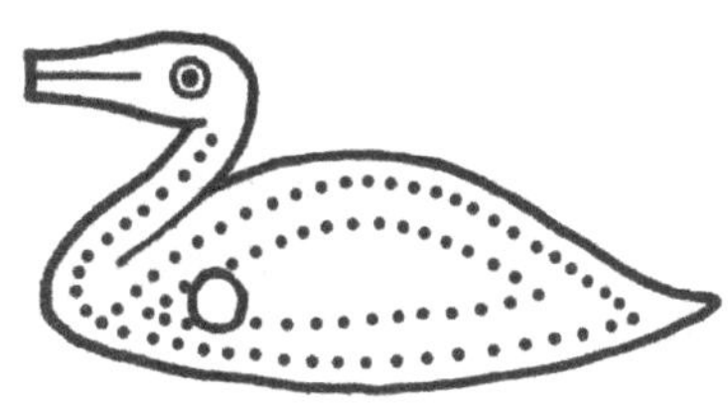

177 (left) – Clasp in the shape of a bird of prey from the West-Gothic tomb of a woman No. 756 of Vicq (Yvelines), 5th-6th c. [12.86-88, Fig. 23]

178 (right) – as in 176, [11.Table 19, Fig. 196; 10.17, Fig. 196]

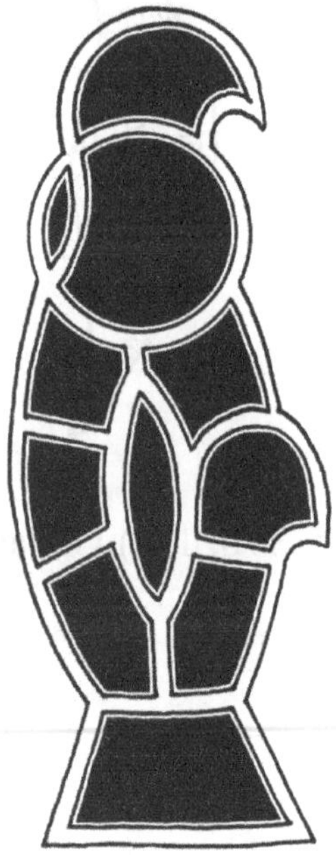

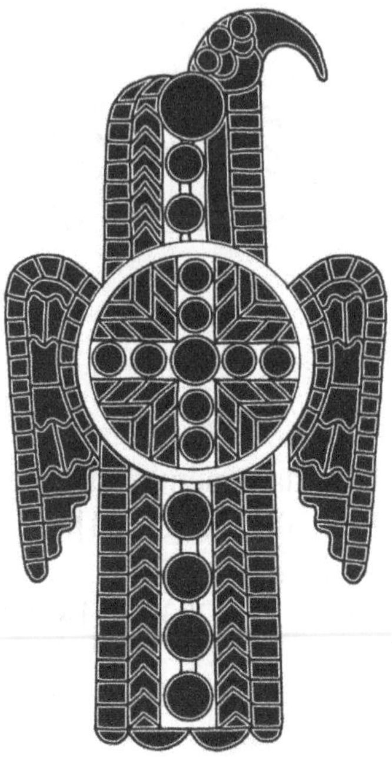

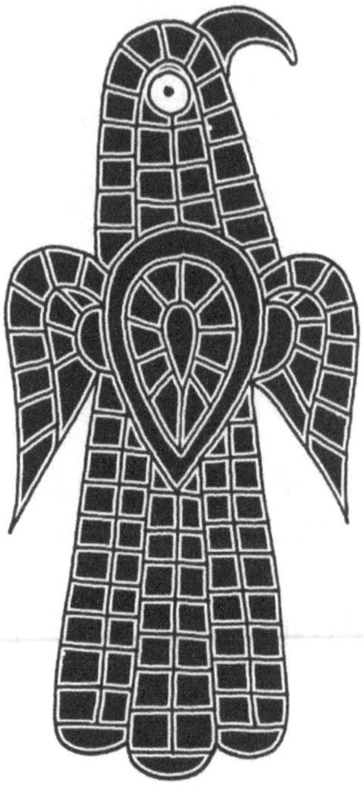

179 – Gold bird-shaped fibula adorned with red and blue enamel, from the Schwabmünchen burial site in Germany [3. Fig. 123]

180 – Eagle-shaped brooch – a typical Ostrogoth motif taken over by the Franks. Almost identical brooches are found in France, Spain, Italy, and San Marino. Ca. 500 CE [3. dwg. 126]

181 – Germanic eagle-shaped brooch – a typical Ostrogoth motif taken over by the Franks [3. dwg. 126]

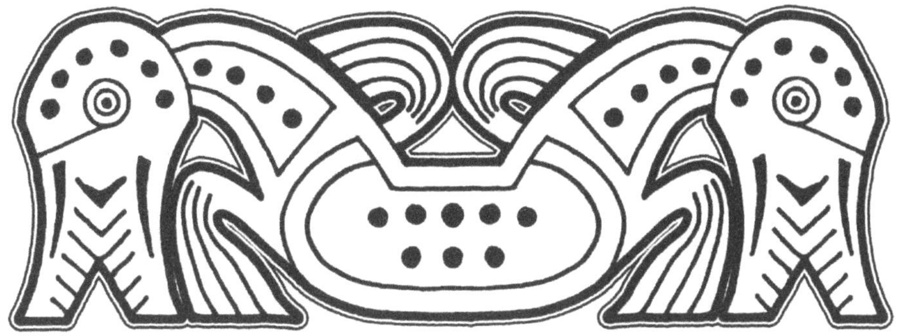

182 – Two animal figures in Style II on a rectangular belt strap plate. Gotland, ca. 550-600 CE [11. Table 31, Fig. 338; 10.22, Fig. 338]

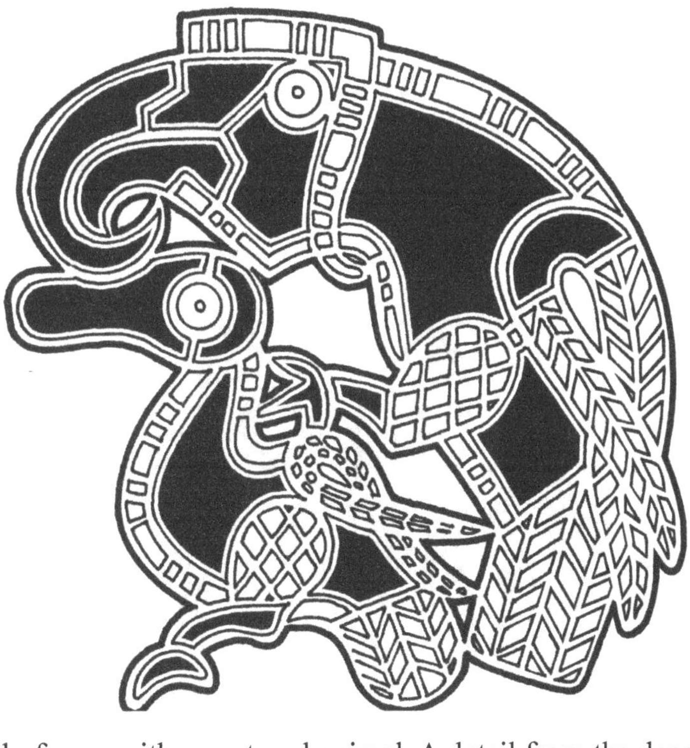

183 – Bird of prey with a captured animal. A detail from the decorations of the Sutton Hoo purse (See 047) presented in 086, [4.87-88, plate VIII; 18.34]

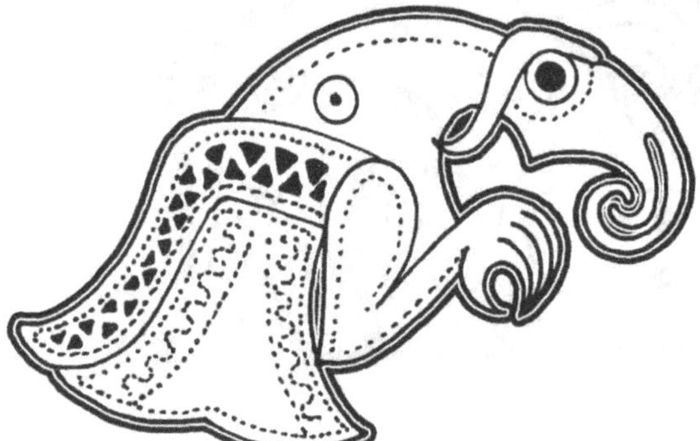

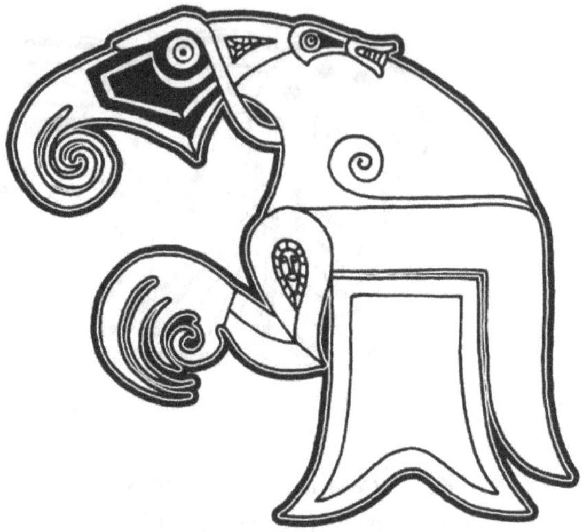

184 (left) – Bird of prey-shaped fibula. Gotland, ca. 550-600 CE [11.Table. 13, Fig. 109; 10.15, Fig. 109]

185 (right) – A bird of prey (Raven? Eagle?) ornament adorning the shield from Mound 1 ship burial at Sutton Hoo (for information on the burial see No. 047). Its head and legs are bronze, while the body and tail were made from gold foil (For a detail from the figure of the bird see No. 079), [4.49-55, Fig. 35]

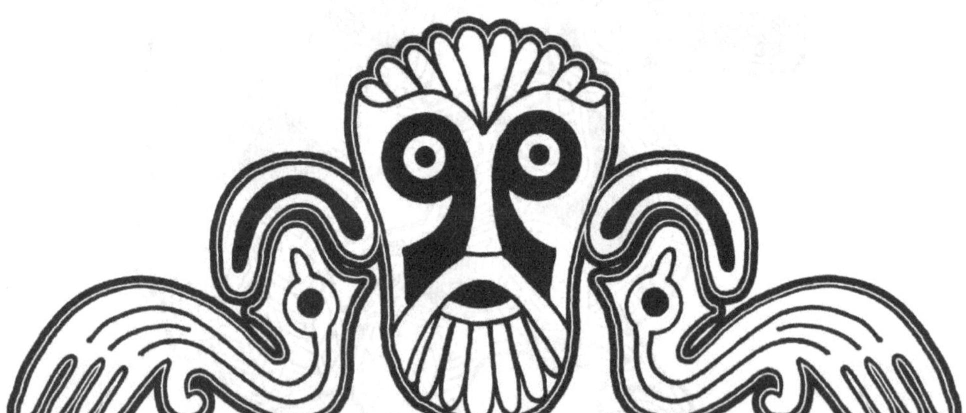

186 – Bearded man mask on the upper guard of a sword from the Staffordshire Hoard (For an ornament on the second side of the head, see No. 125, and for the ornament see No. 102) [9108; http://www.staffordshirehoard.org.uk/gallery/swords]

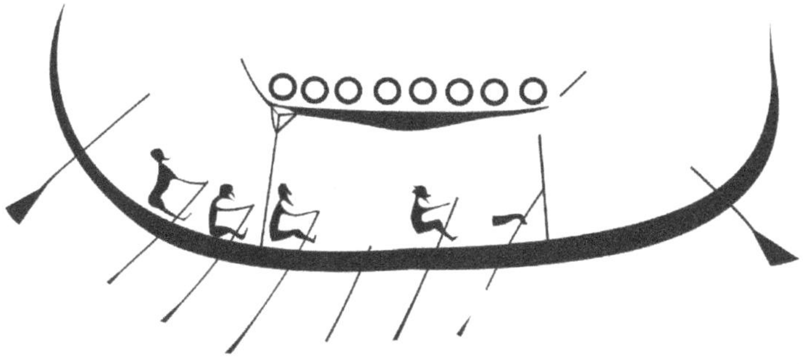

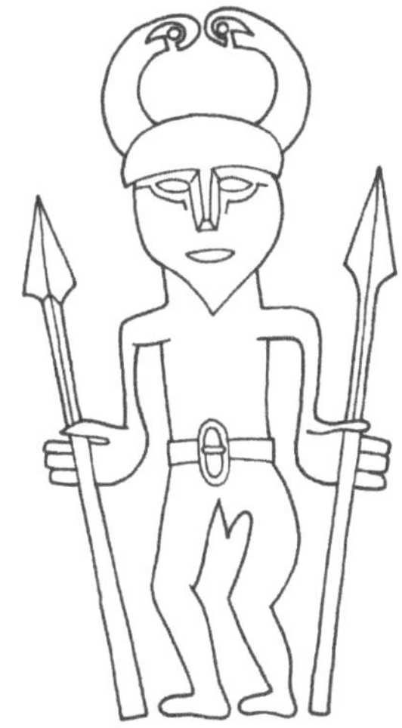

187 (left) – Rowed ship on one of the early Gotland curved picture stones, Sanda church. Such boats are present on other stones of that early series. For other details from the same Stone, see No. 020, 244, and 245 [15.303-304, Fig. 11]

188 (right) – Naked warrior clad only in a belt and helmet with bird head terminals, dancing with two spears. A relief in gilded copper alloy on a belt buckle from the male grave 95, Finglesham, Kent (England). The image refers to the well-known representations from Sweden, 7th c. [17.41, Fig. 22, 14.18, 17, plate 13]

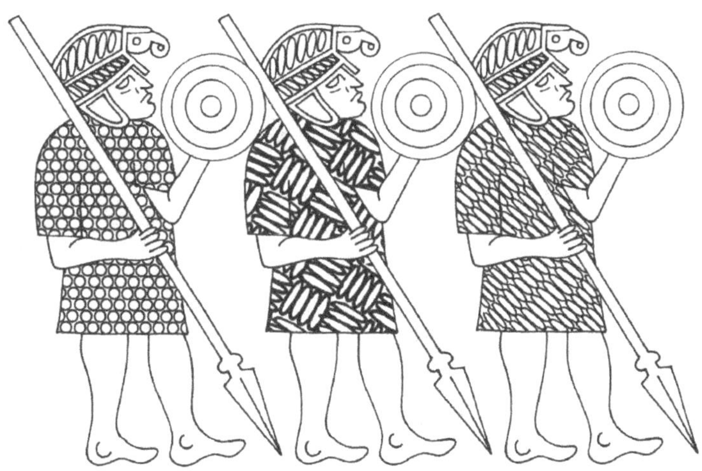

189 – Example of representation of a procession of warriors. Themes such as this are translated as the Einherier (fallen warriors accompanying Odin in Valhalla and at Ragnarök), a ritual dance of warriors, or a warband before a battle. The warriors, as described much earlier by Tacitus (1st cent. CE) sing, using their shields held against their mouths as resonators to amplify their voices. Embossment on a pressblech of the Valsgärde 7 helmet (See 081) (For another motif from the same helmet see below – 190) [9.54-61, P14A]

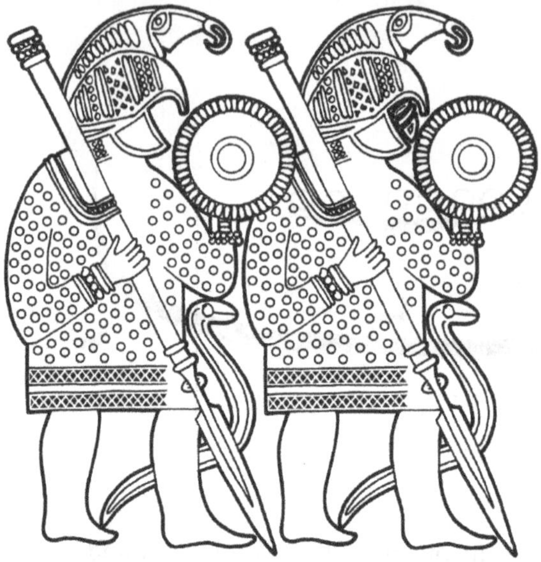

190 – One more motif with warriors (in this case two) dressed in wrap around kytels, armor (byrnies), and helmets topped with heads of birds of prey, wielding spears and shields raised to the height of their heads. In front of each a serpent is shown (representing the underworld powers). Embossment on a pressblech of the Valsgärde 7 helmet (See 081). For a different theme from the same helmet see above under No. 189. [14.17, No. 15, plate 12]

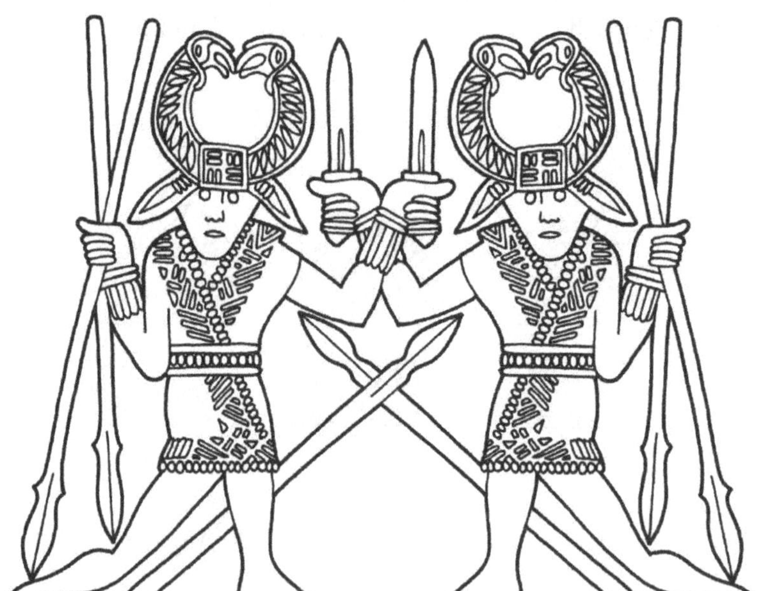

191 – The Dancing Man motif, depicting warriors dressed as their Swedish equivalents in wraparound kytels and headgear topped with bird head terminals, performing a dance with weapons (spears and swords). Embossed bronze plate of a decorative helmet from Sutton Hoo (See No. 047). A very similar representation is found on the Valsgärde 7 helmet (See No. 189 and 190), [4.46-49, Plate III, 14.13, No. 10, Plate 8]

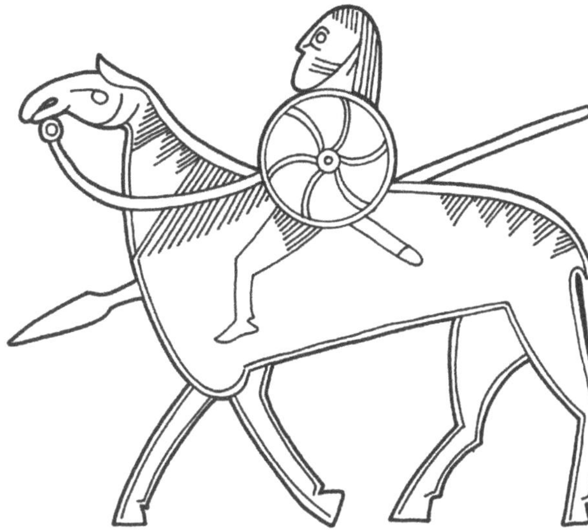

192 – Horseback warrior armed with a spear and shield depicted on the Hornhausen stela. For other details from this stone see No. 024 and 187, [3. dwg. 107]

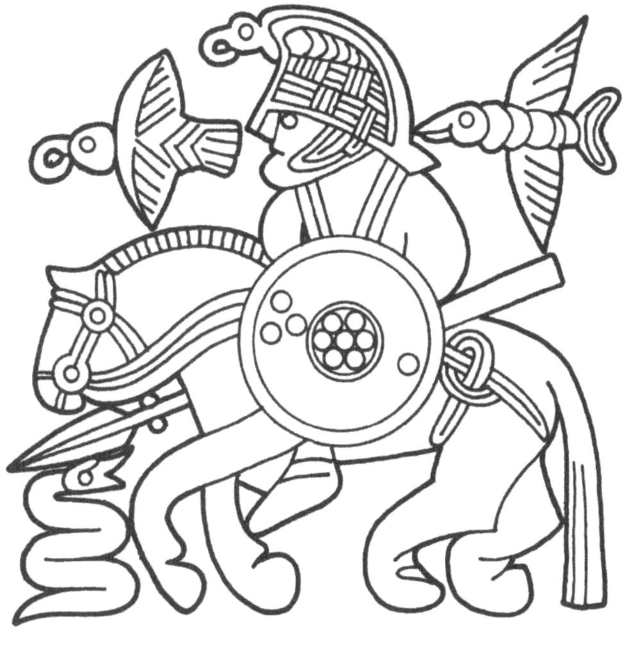

193 – Odin riding a horse, wearing a bird crested helmet, armed with a spear and a shield, and accompanied by two birds – probably the ravens Hugginn and Muninn (Thought and Memory) and a snake, embossed on a decorative plaque (pressbleck) adorning the helmet from the Vendel 1 grave (see No. 59) [14.16, No. 15, plate 11]

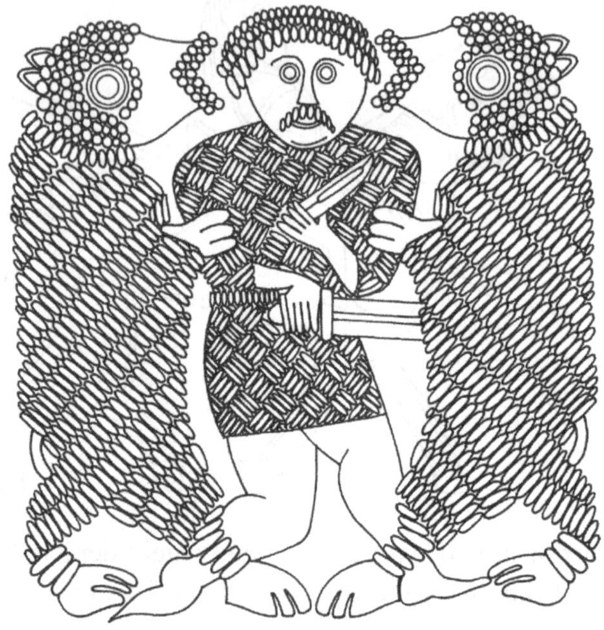

194 – Merovingian signet ring celebrating a betrothal, signed with the names Dromacius and Betta. Mulsanne, Sarthe (France), 6th-7th c. [British Museum]

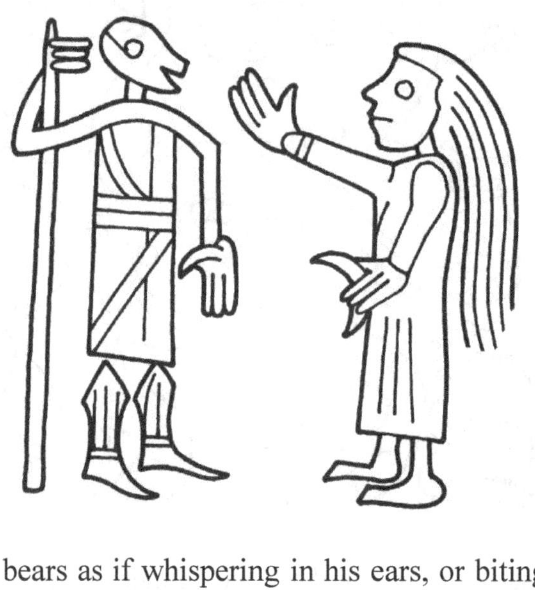

195 – Warrior and two bears as if whispering in his ears, or biting his head. The warrior holds a knife in one hand, and a sword in the other, stabbing the belly of one of the beasts. One of the four bronze die stamping plates used for decorating helmets (so-called pressblech) from Torslunda, Öland (Sweden), 6th c. (See 201 for a similar theme, for another form from the same site see 197) [4117, Fig. 97; 14.13, nr 9, Plate 7]

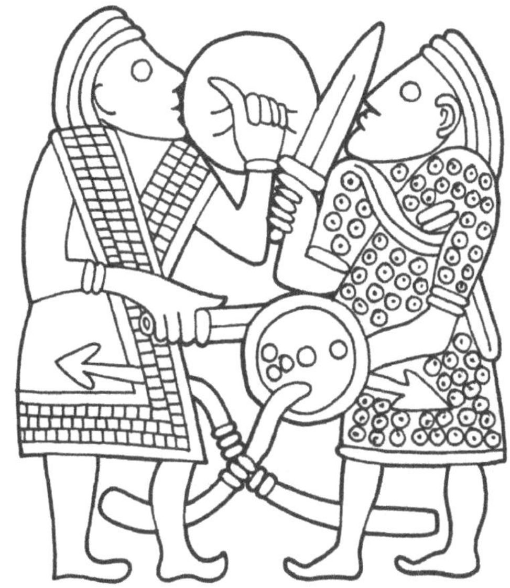

196 – Fighting warriors, one of whom wears a distinctive jacket (wrap around kytel) and the other – chainmail and other armor (byrnie). They fight with swords, but they had cast their javelins to the ground. One was stabbed in the shield, while the other's kytel was pierced. Scene embossed on a pressblech adorning the helmet from Vendel grave 14, (see No. 059) [14.16, No. 15, plate 11]

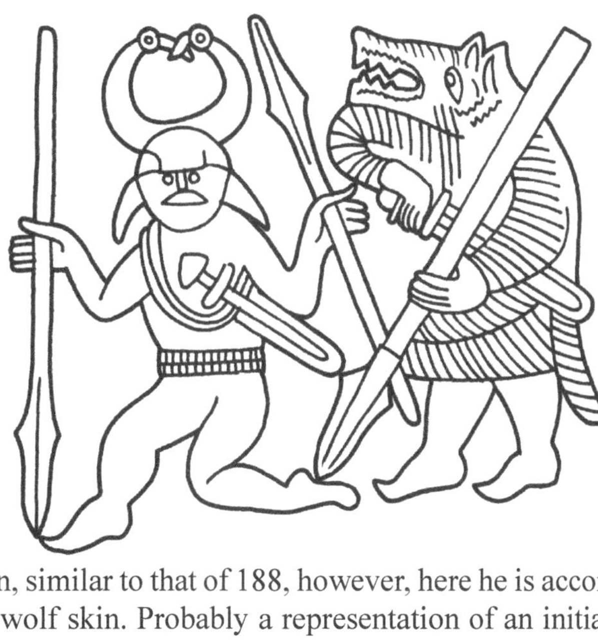

197 – Dancing Man, similar to that of 188, however, here he is accompanied by another warrior wearing a wolf skin. Probably a representation of an initiation rite associated with transcending the human condition and the society to enter into a particular group of warriors (Ulfhednar) (Also see below – No. 198, for another form from the same location see No. 195), 6th c. [4.117, Fig. 97; 14.13, nr 9, Plate 7]

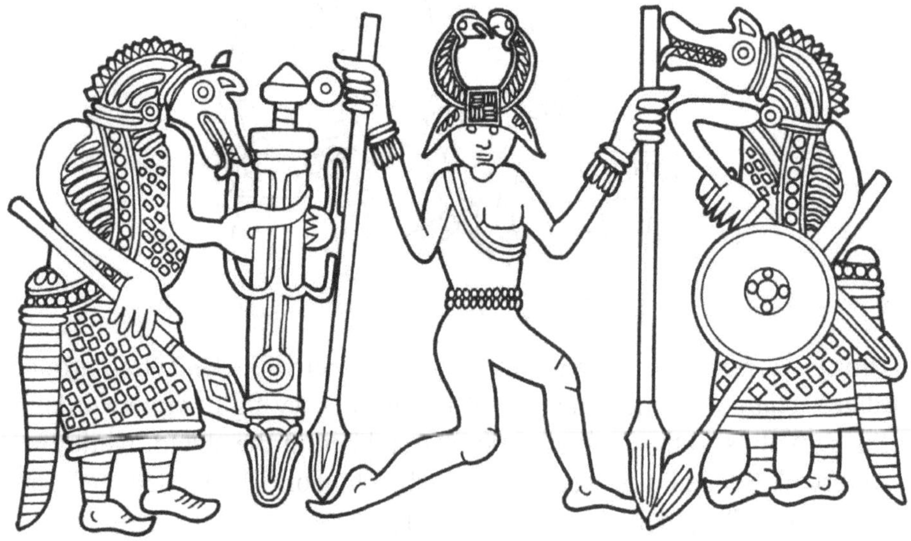

198 – One more Dancing Man again, this time between two warriors clad in wolf skins (Ulfhednir, See above: 197), each armed with a shield, spear and a sword, in one case a very distinctive ring pommel sword, possessed only by elite warriors of the guard. The Dancing Man again is armed with two spears and appears to be naked except for a horned helmet and a belt, which is a development of the theme from the silver scabbard fittings from the Church of St. Gallas, Gutenstein (Germany), 7th c. [14.23, No. 32; 9.52]

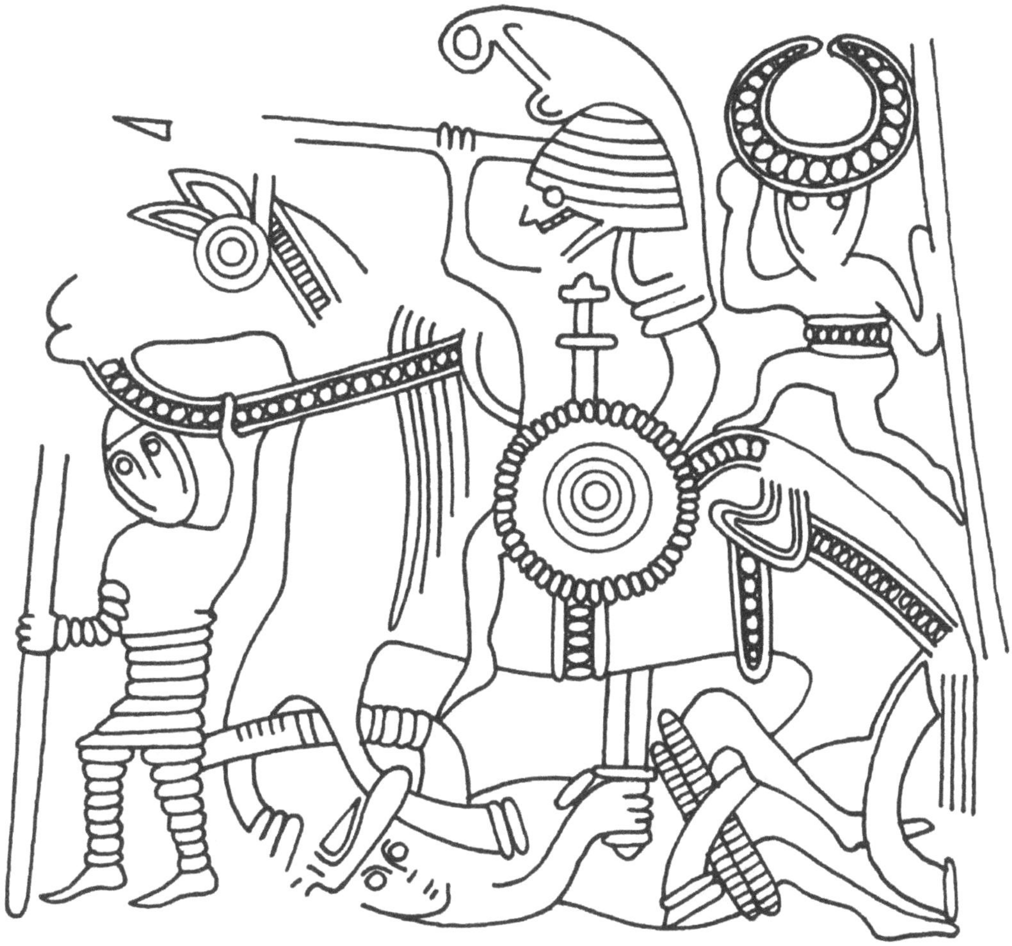

199 – Warrior on horseback wearing a bird crested helmet charges at his opponent with a raised spear. Behind him stands a small figure, naked except for a belt and helmet with horns with bird head terminals, who also holds the yore of his spear as if in a gesture of guidance. Another warrior, trampled by thc horse's hooves, thrusts a sword into its belly. Before him, another figure armed with a spear holds the horse's bridle. Representation on a pressblech from the Valsgärde grave 8 (See No. 081) (A very similar theme see is shown below under No. 200) [14.17, No. 15, Plate 12]

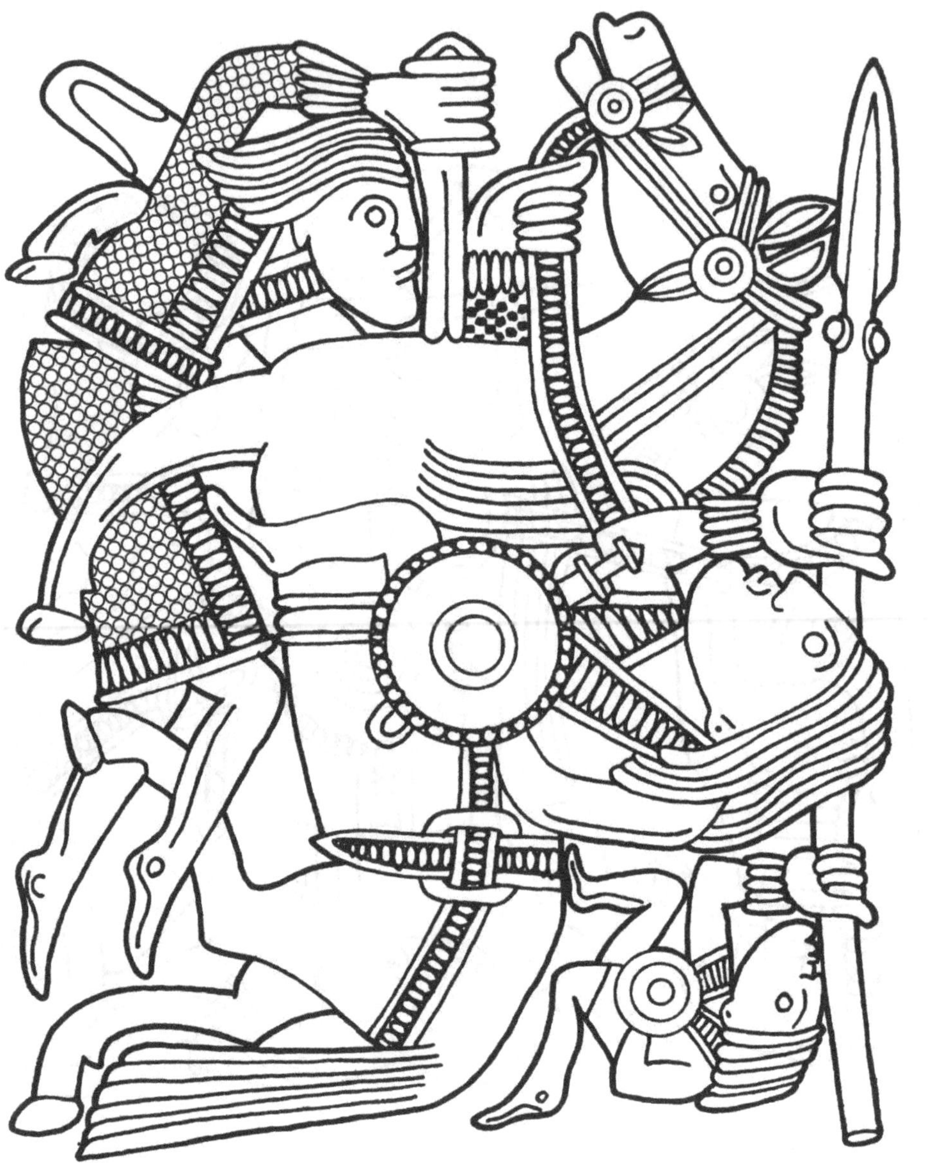

200 – Much the same theme as above (No. 199), with the difference that the figures' heads are bare, and that the trampled on warriors stabs the horse and holds the bridle as well [4.4649, Plate III]

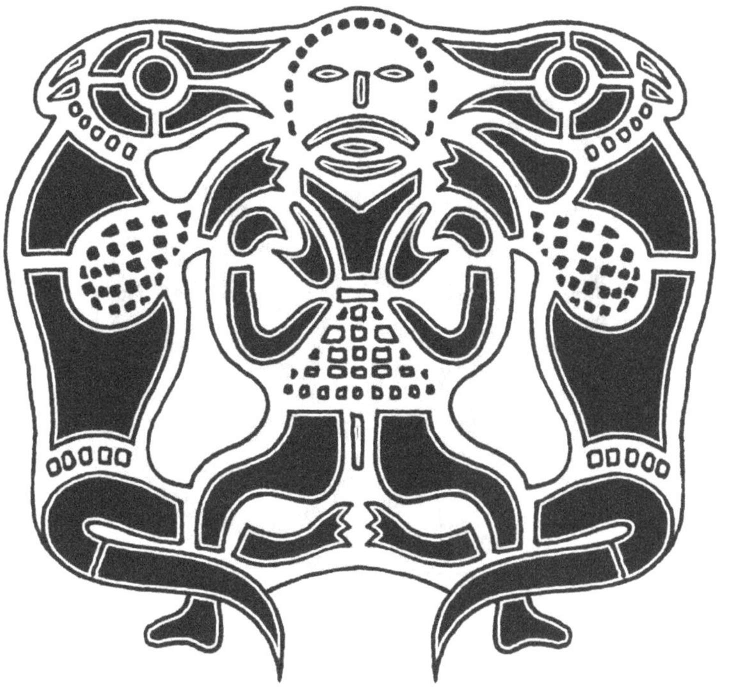

201 – Man and two bears – or similar beasts – on his left and right, biting him, or whispering to him (See No. 086) (For a similar theme see 195) [4.87-88, plate VIII]

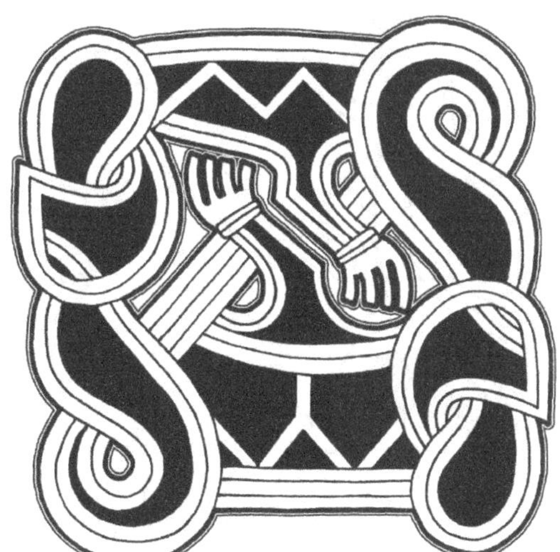

202 – Animal Style I pattern from the gold plate grips of the sword from Grave V, Snartemo Hägebostad, Vest Agder, Norway. Early 6th c. CE (See No. 025) [Museum of Cultural History Oslo]

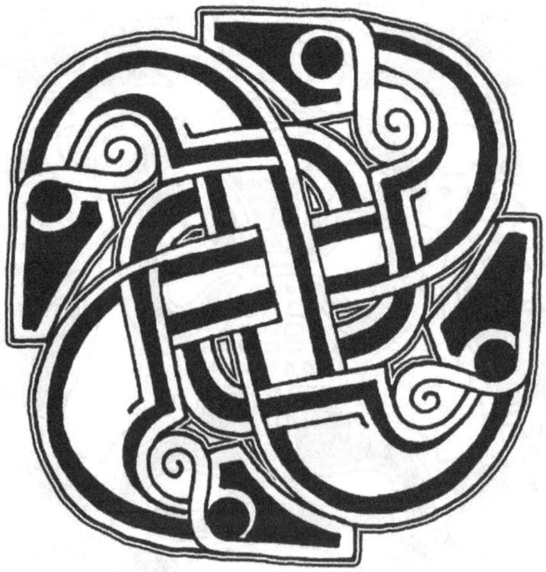

203 – Animal Style II pattern on a square, bronze fitting on a harness, arranged in a swastika motif. Gotland, ca. 550-600 CE [11.Table 80, Fig. 692; 10.32, Fig. 692]

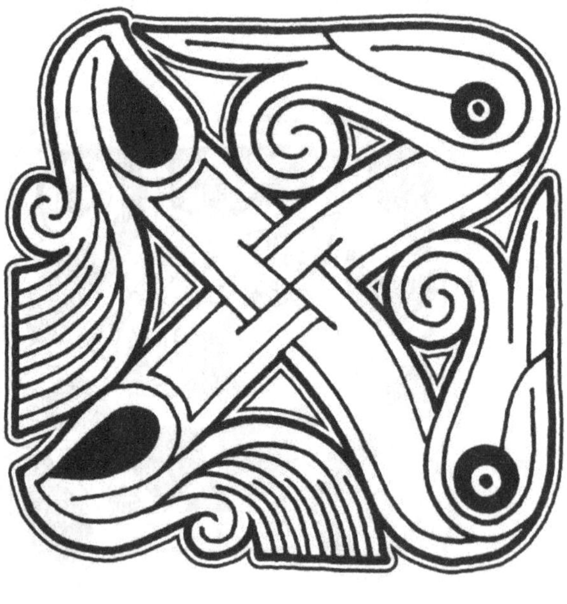

204 – As above. [11.Table 80, Fig. 693; 10.32, Fig. 693]

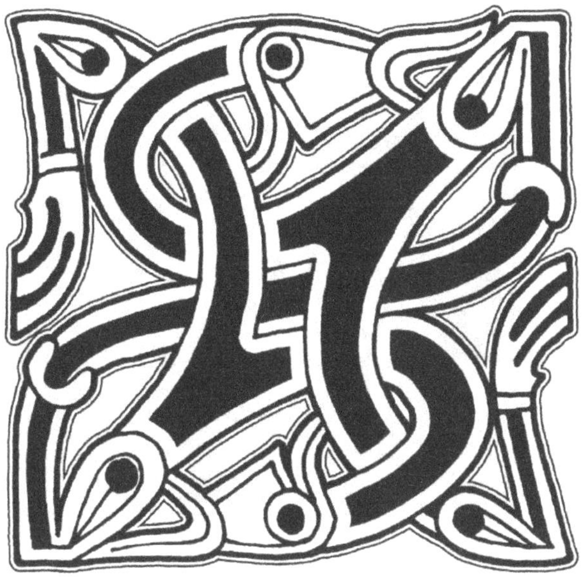

205 – As above. [11.Table 81, Fig. 700; 10.32, Fig. 700]

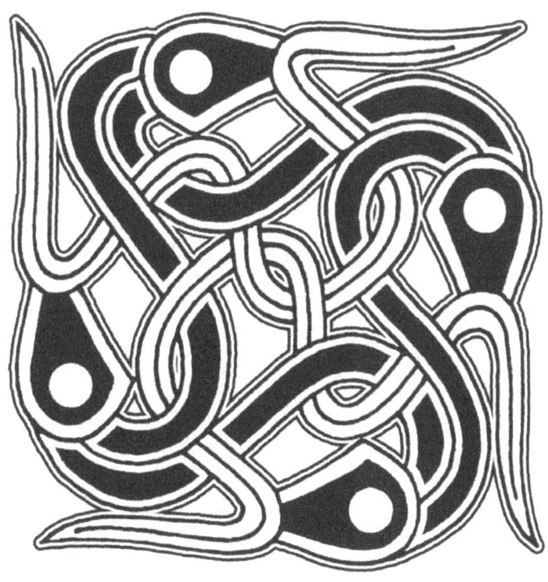

206 – As above. [11.Table 81, Fig. 694; 10.32, Fig. 694]

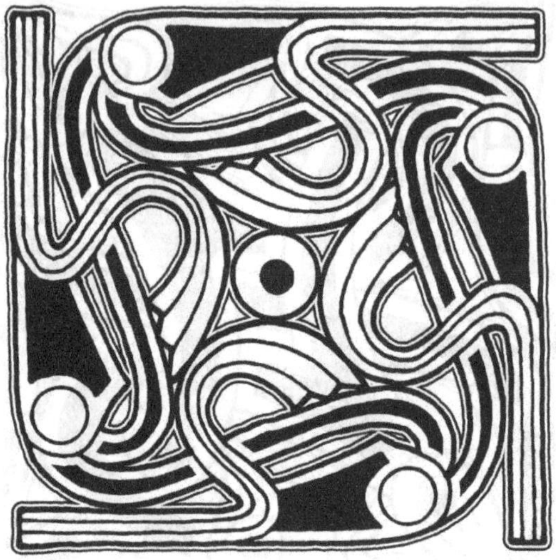

207 – As above. [11.Table 81, Fig. 695; 10.32, Fig. 695]

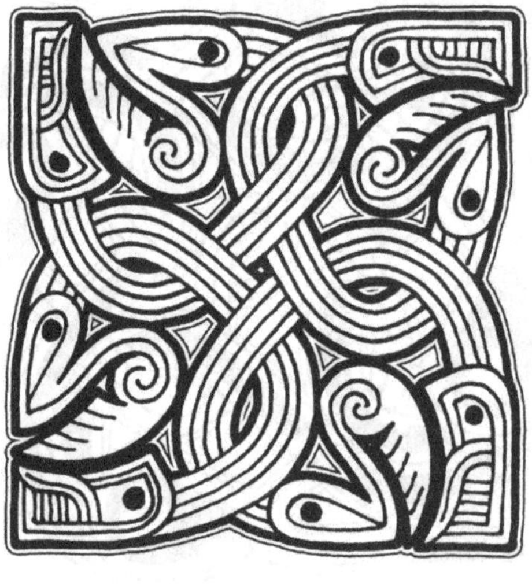

208 – As above. [11.Table 81, Fig. 696; 10.32, Fig. 696]

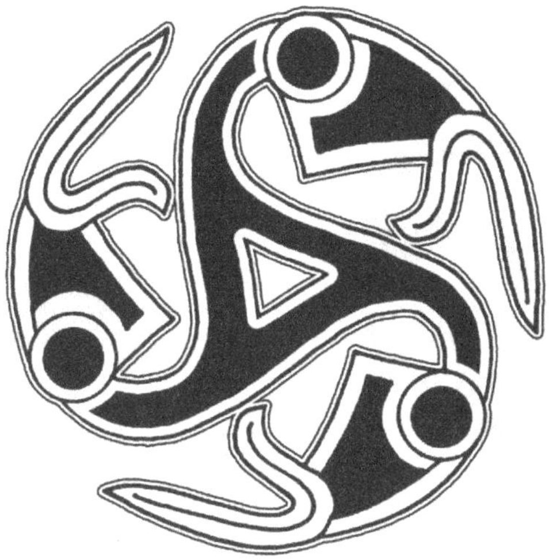

209 – Four zoomorphic figures in early Animal Style II arranged in a triskelion on sword and sheath. Gotland, ca. 550-600 CE [11.Table 55, Fig. 534; 10.28, Fig. 534]

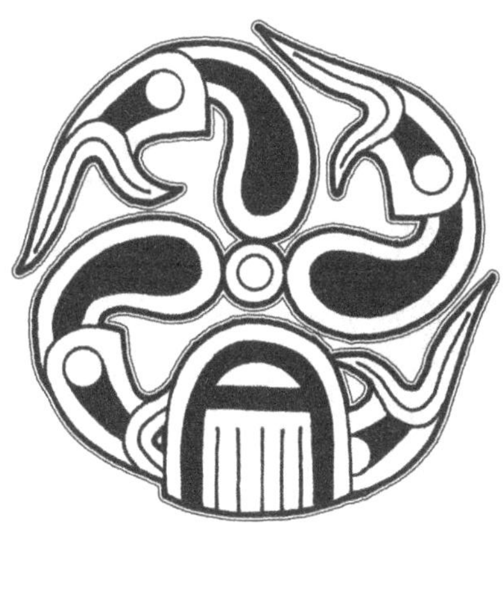

210 – Zoomorphic figures in late Animal Style II arranged in a swastika on a brakteat. Gotland, ca. 650-700 CE [11.Table 177, Fig. 1475; 10.54, Fig. 1475]

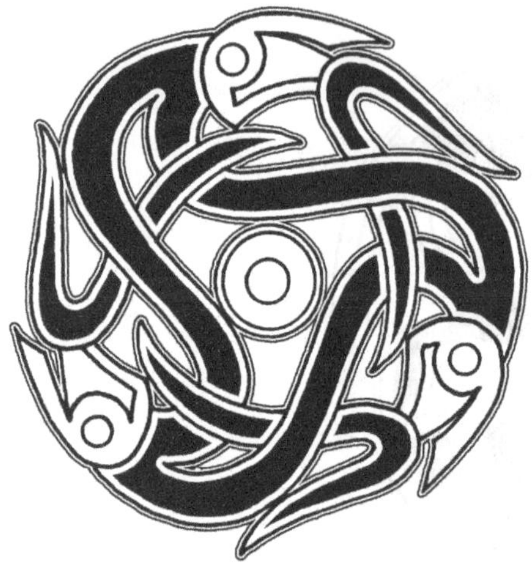

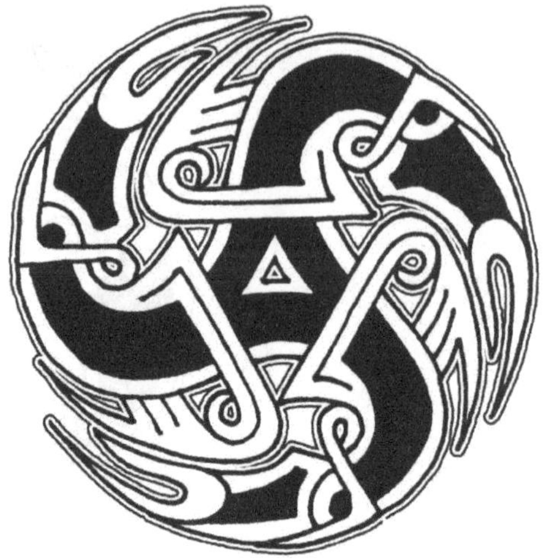

211 (left) – Zoomorphic figures in early Animal Style II arranged in a triskelion on a round fibula. Gotland, ca. 550-600 CE [11.Table 11, Fig. 82; 10.14, Fig. 82]

212 (right) – Zoomorphic figures in early Animal Style II arranged in a triskelion on a bronze overlay on an iron rivet from a shield. Gotland, ca. 550-600 CE [11.Table 75, Fig. 660; 10.31, Fig. 660]

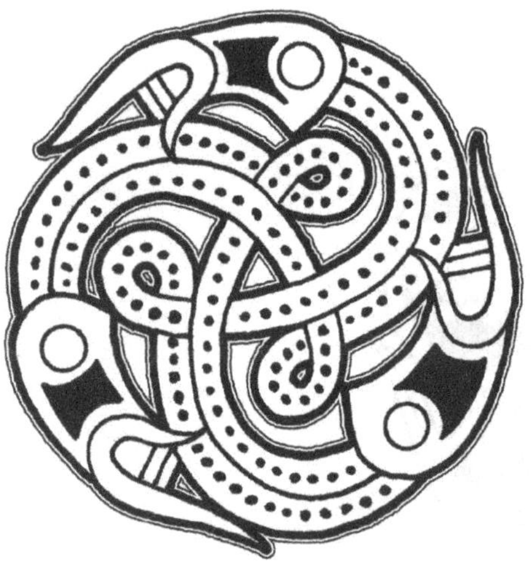

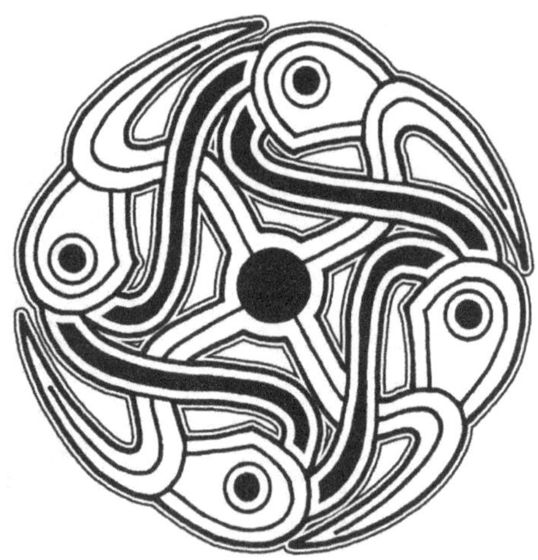

213 (left) – as in No. 211 [11.Table 11, Fig. 90; 10.15, Fig. 90]

214 (right) – Zoomorphic figures in early Animal Style II arranged in a swastika on a decorative rivet on the flat surface of a shield boss. Gotland, ca. 550-600 CE [11. Table 71, Fig. 634; 10.30, Fig. 634]

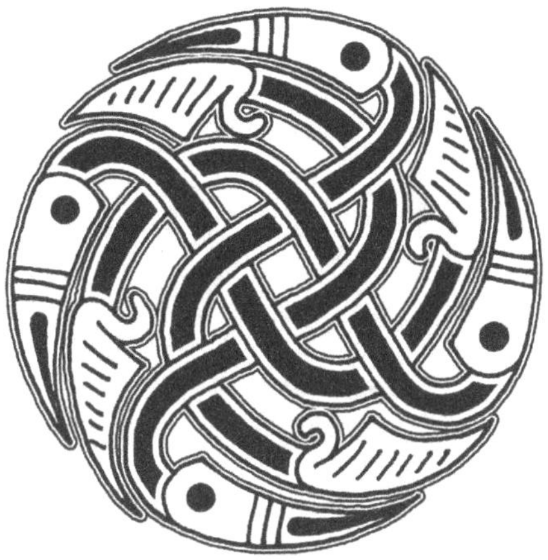

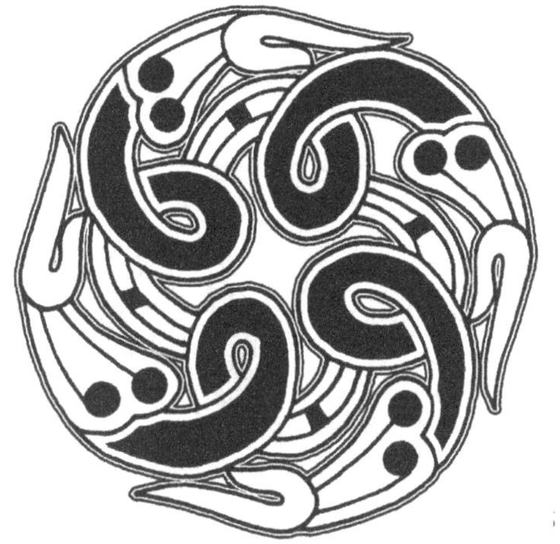

215 (left) – Zoomorphic figures in early Animal Style II arranged in a swastika on a decorative rivet on the flat surface of a shield boss. Gotland, ca. 550-600 CE [11.Table 75, Fig. 662; 10.31, Fig. 662]

216 (right) – Zoomorphic figures in early Animal Style II arranged in a swastika on a decorative rivet on the flat surface of a shield boss. Gotland, ca. 550-600 CE [11.Table 71, Fig. 636; 10.30, Fig. 636]

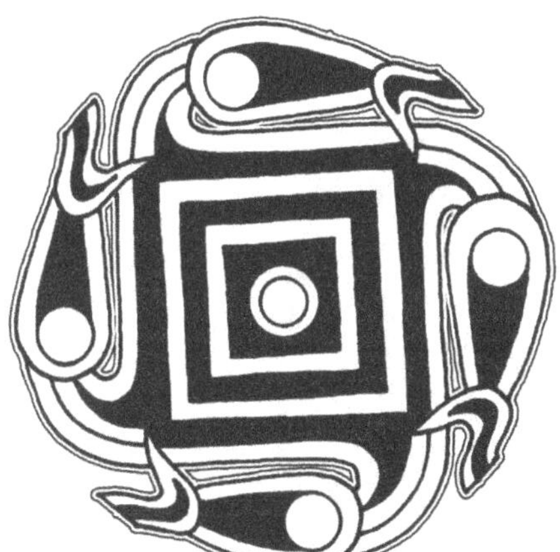

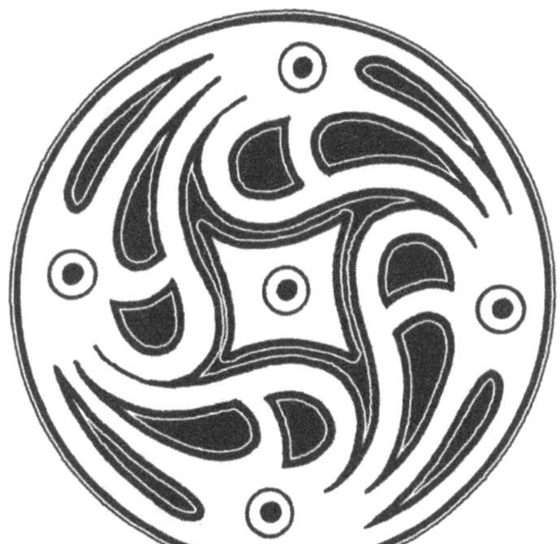

217 (left) – Four animal heads in early Animal Style II on a round fibula. Originally, carbuncles were set as the eyes. Gotland, ca. 550-600 CE [11.Table 11, Fig. 89; 10.15, Fig. 89]

218 (right) – Four zoomorphic figures in early Animal Style II arranged in a swastika on a round fibula. Gotland, ca. 550-600 CE [11.Table 11, Fig. 84; 10.15, Fig. 84]

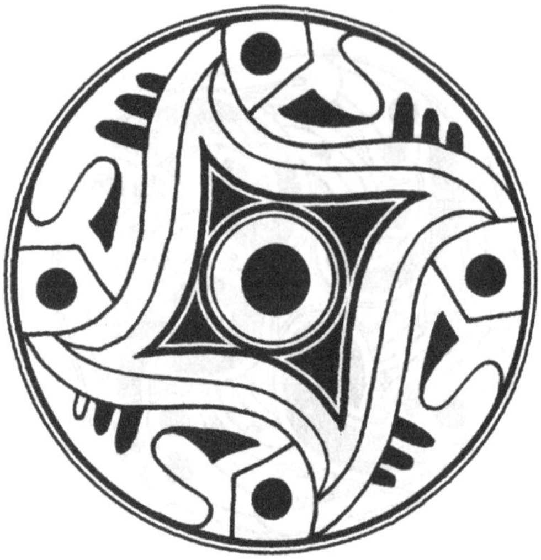

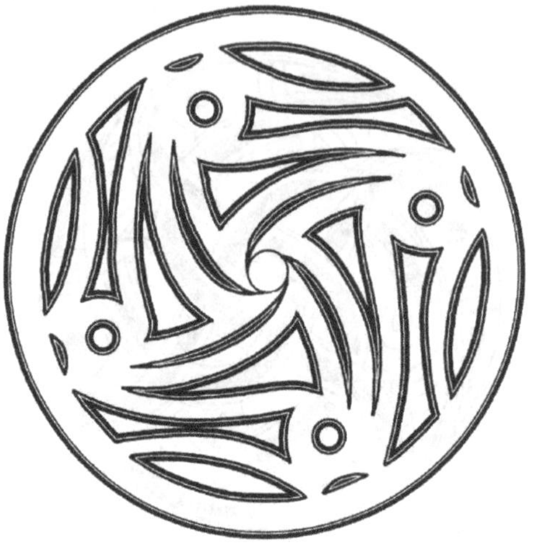

219 (left) – As above. [11.Table 11, Fig. 85; 10.15, Fig. 85]

220 (right) – Swastika motif on a bronze, tinned plaque on the bottom of one of the three Celtic hanging bronze bowls found in a Sutton Hoo burial (see 047). The Celtic ornamentation is completely different from the style of most objects deposited in the grave [4.72-75, Fig. 57, British Museum]

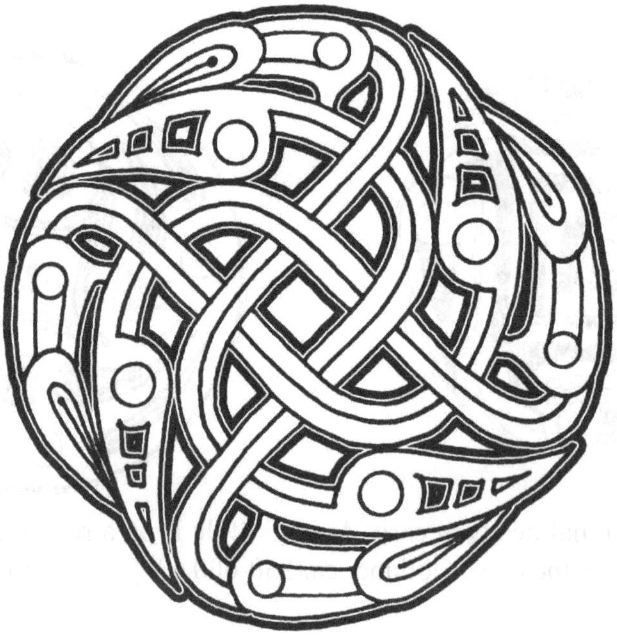

221 – as under No. 218 [11.Table 11, Fig. 87; 10.15, Fig. 87]

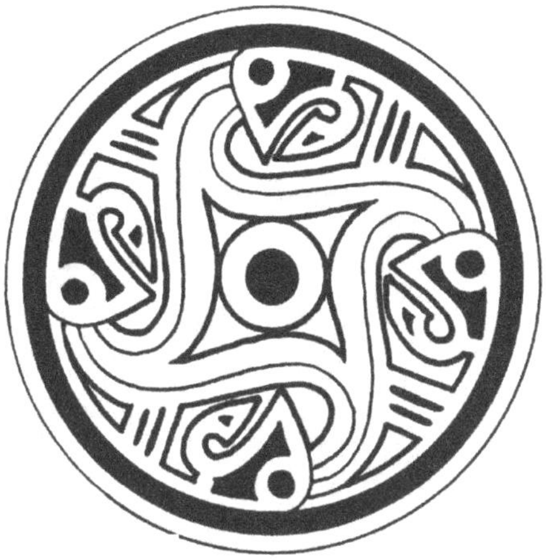

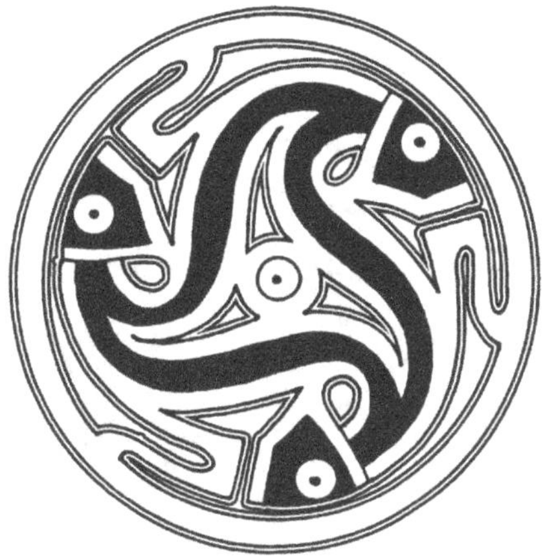

222 (left) –Animal Style II figures arranged in a swastika on a round fibula. Gotland, ca. 600-650 CE [11.Table 104, Fig. 877; 10.37, Fig. 877]

223 (right) – Animal Style III figures arranged in a triskelion on a round fibula. Gotland, ca. 600-650 CE [11.Table 104, Fig. 872; 10.37, Fig. 872]

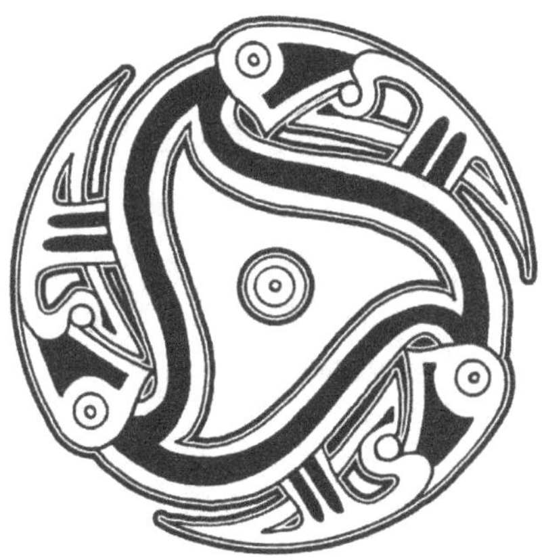

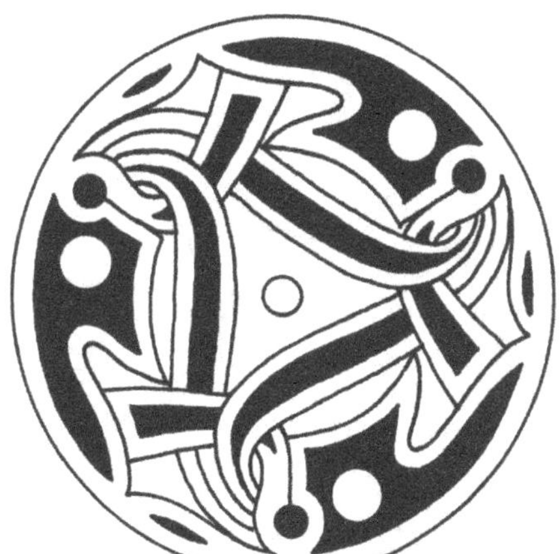

224 (left) – As above. [11.Table 104, Fig. 874; 10.37, Fig. 874]

225 (right) – Zoomorphic figures arranged in a triskelion on a round fibula. Gotland, ca. 650-700 CE [11.Table 167, Fig. 1386; 10.52, Fig. 1386]

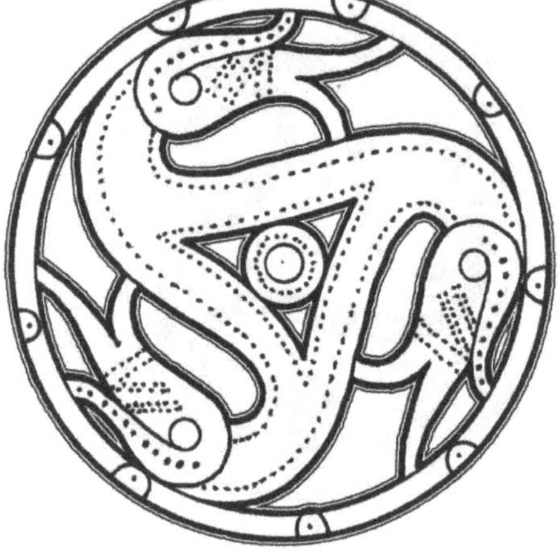

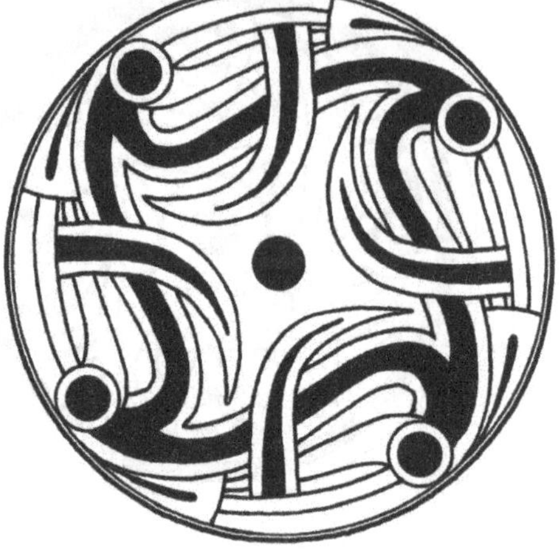

226 (left) – Cut-work panel with three Animal Style II figures. Gotland, ca. 600-650 CE [11.Table 113, Fig. 977; 10.39, Fig. 977]

227 (right) – Early Animal Style II figures arranged in a swastika on a round fibula. Gotland, ca. 600-650 CE [11.Table 105, Fig. 886; 10.37, Fig. 886]

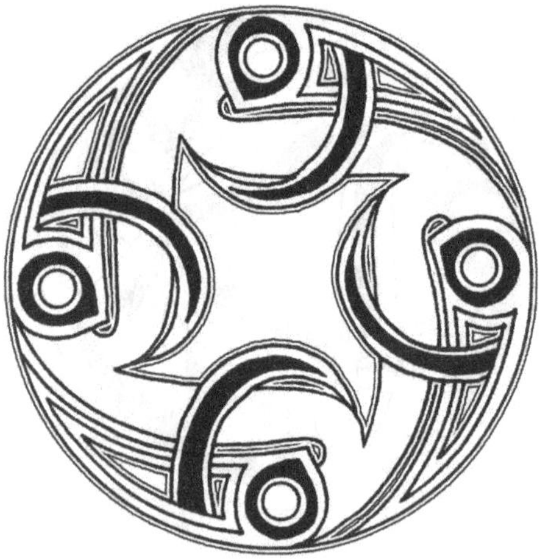

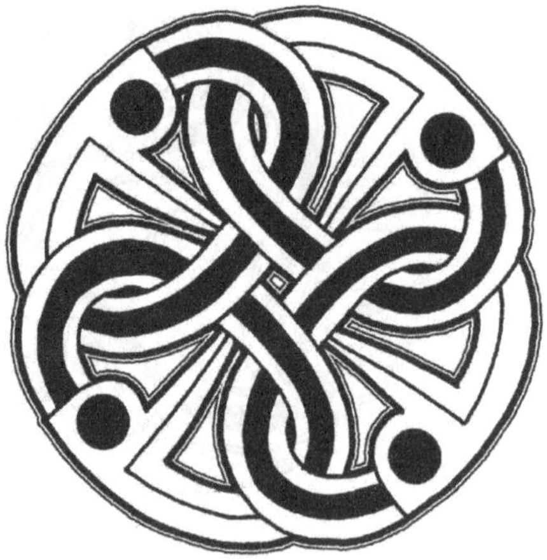

228 (left) – Early Animal Style II figures arranged in a swastika on a round fibula. Gotland, ca. 650-700 CE [11.Table 168, Fig. 1399; 10.53, Fig. 1399]

229 (right) – As above, Gotland, ca. 600-650 CE, [11.Table. 105, Fig. 890; 10.37, Fig. 890]

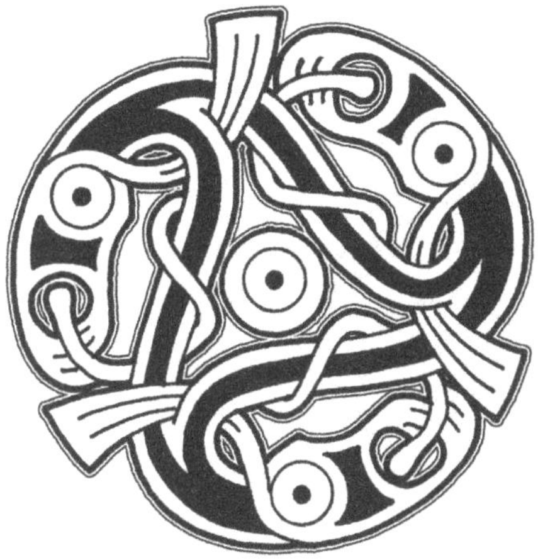

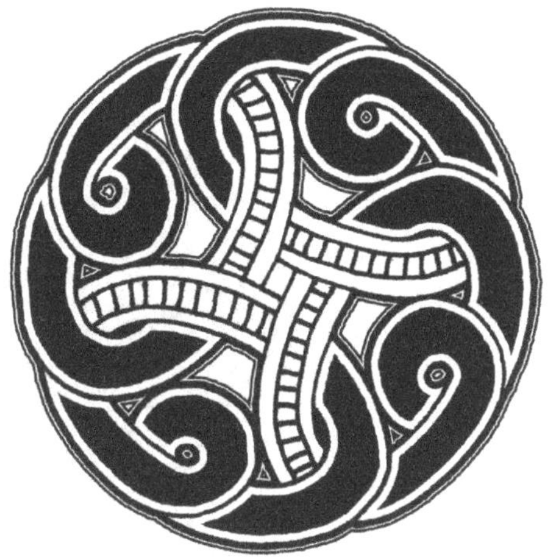

230 (left) – Animal Style III figures arranged in a triskelion on a round fibula. Gotland, ca. 700-750 CE [11.Table 221, Fig. 1807; 10.65, Fig. 1807]

231 (right) – Ornament on a round fibula. Gotland, ca. 550-600 CE, [11.Table. 11, Fig. 91; 10.15, Fig. 91]

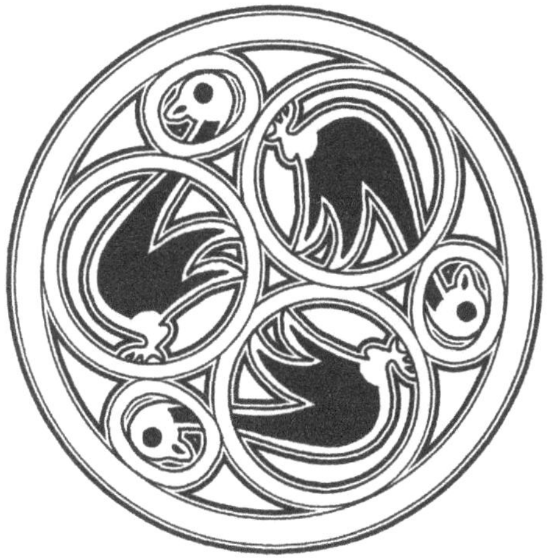

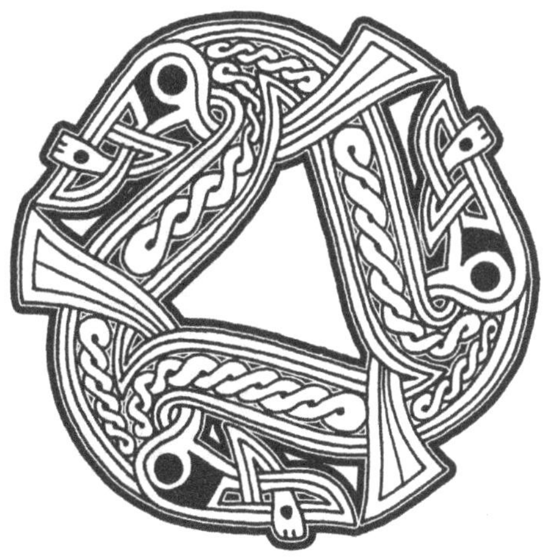

232 (left) – Cut-work panel with more realistic animal figures suggesting Style III. Gotland, ca. 700-750 CE [11.Table 228, Fig. 1880; 10.67, Fig. 1880]

233 (right) – Late Animal Style II figures decorated with plait patterns and arranged in a triskelion on a round fibula. Gotland, ca. 650-700 CE [11.Table 168, Fig. 1392; 10.52, Fig. 1392]

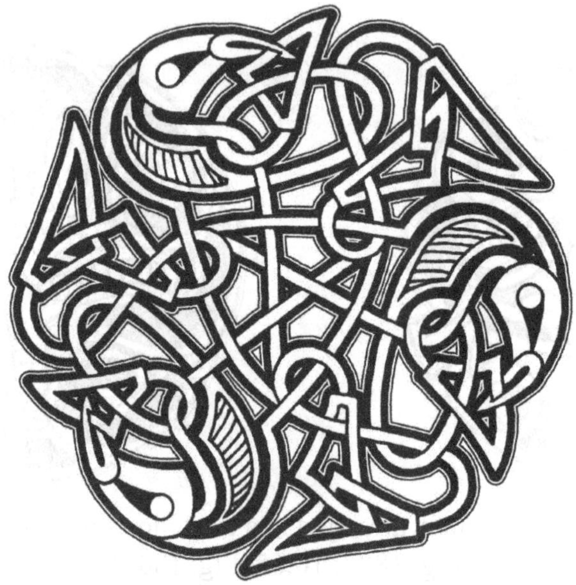

234 – As above, with noteworthy, intricate interlacing animals [11.Table. 168, Fig. 1394; 10.52, Fig. 1394]

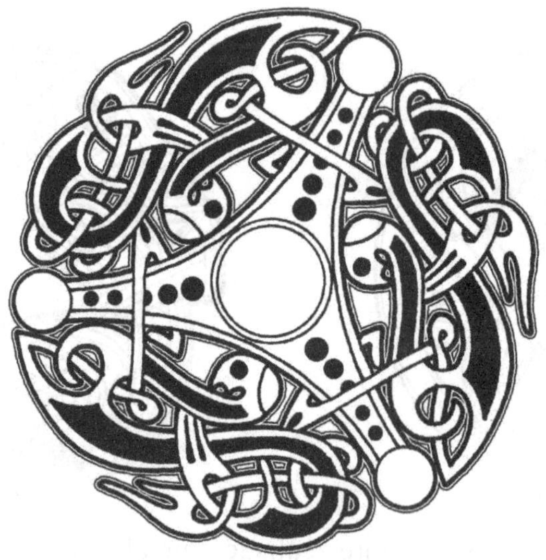

235 – Ornament on a round fibula divided into three sectors filled in by Animal Style III figures. Gotland, ca. 700-750 CE, [11.Table. 223, Fig. 1828; 10.65, Fig. 1828]

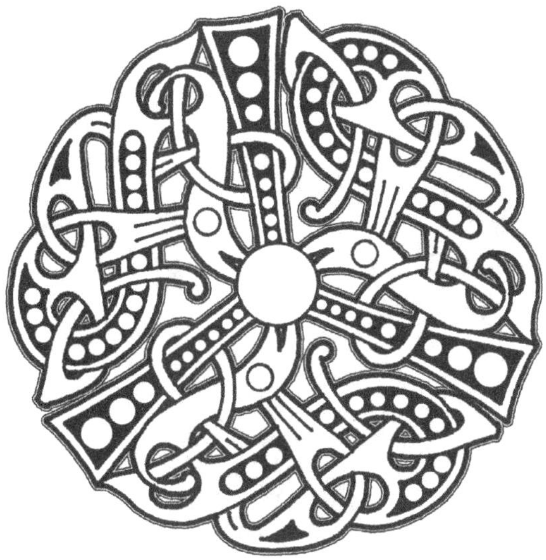

236 – As above. [11.Table 222, Fig. 1821; 10.65, Fig. 1821]

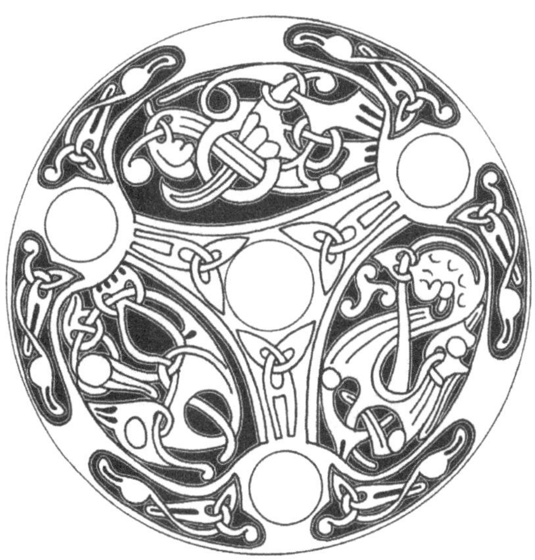

237 – Upper plate of the fibula described under No. 150, completely decorated with animal motifs in Style III

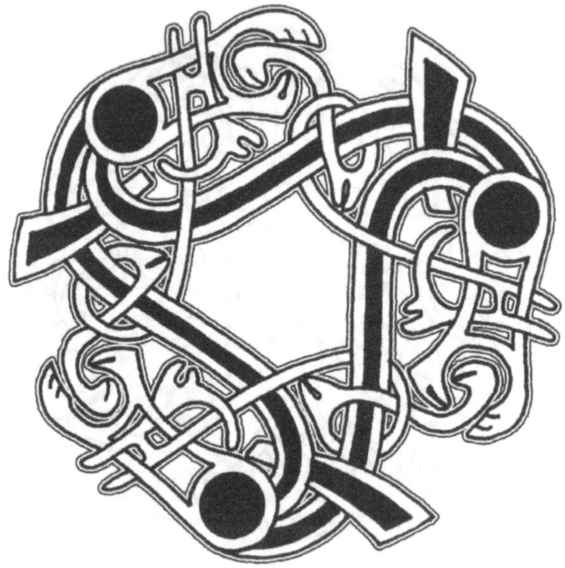

238 – Zoomorphic figures arranged in a triskelion the fibula described under No. 034

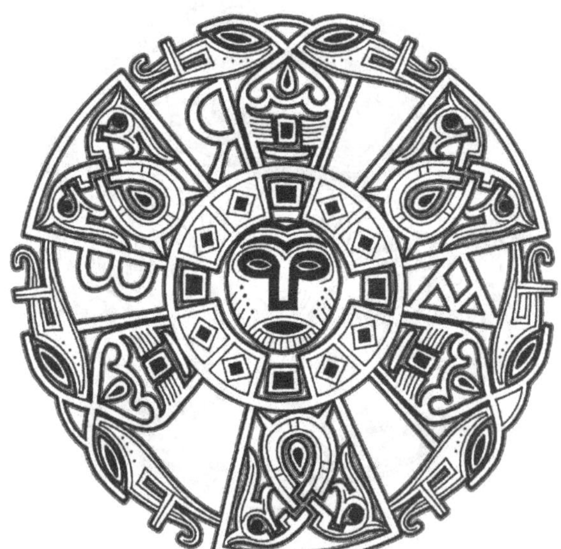

239 – Merovingian plaque associated with Christian worship, although the solar symbolism and influence of barbaric art are all too apparent. Late 6th to early 7th century, Limons (France), [5.48]

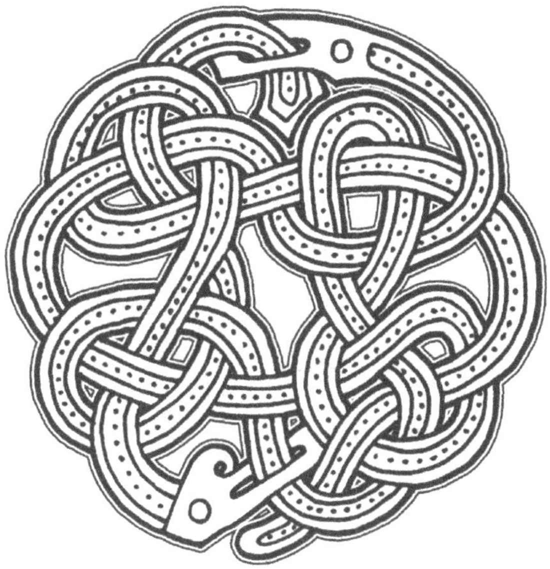

240 – Interlacing animal bodies pattern on the chape of a large belt buckle from Sutto Hoo (See 047) described under No. 089 [4.Plate VII]

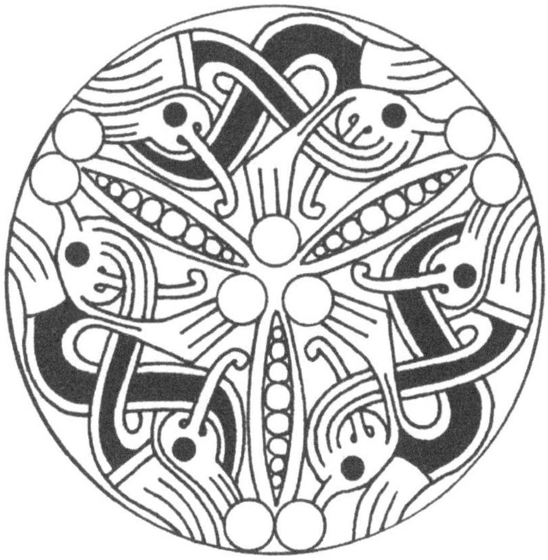

241 – Ornament on a round fibula divided into three sectors filled in by Animal Style III figures. Gotland, ca. 700-750 CE, [11.Table. 222, Fig. 1816; 10.65, Fig. 1816]

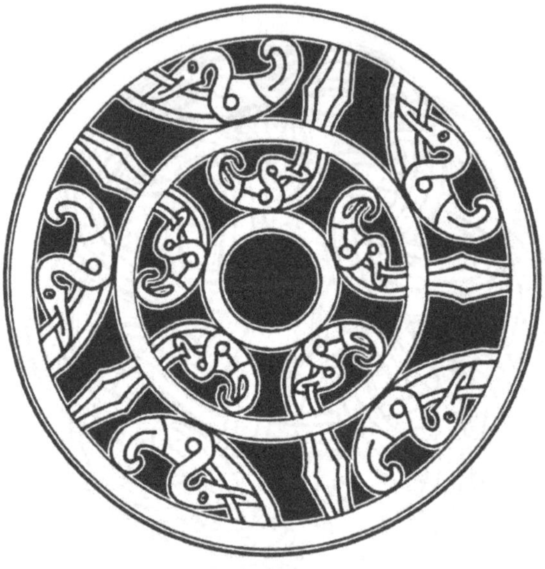

242 – Cut-work panel with ten Animal Style II figures. Gotland, ca. 650-700 CE [11. Table 175, Fig. 1458; 10.54, Fig. 1458]

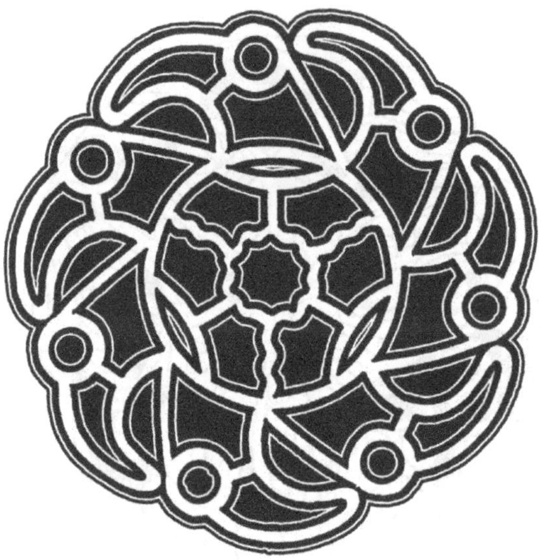

243 – Merovingian fibula from Schwerin-Muess.

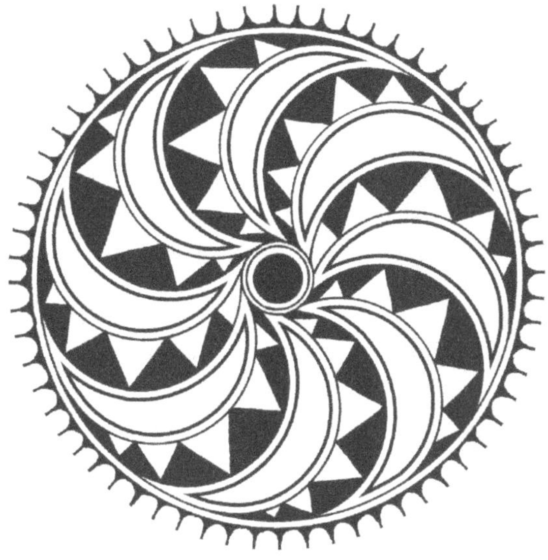

244 – an image of a rowed ship on one of the early Gotland curved picture stone, Sanda church. Such boats are present on other stones of that early series. For other motives from this stone, see: 020, 187, 245 [15.303-304, Fig.11]

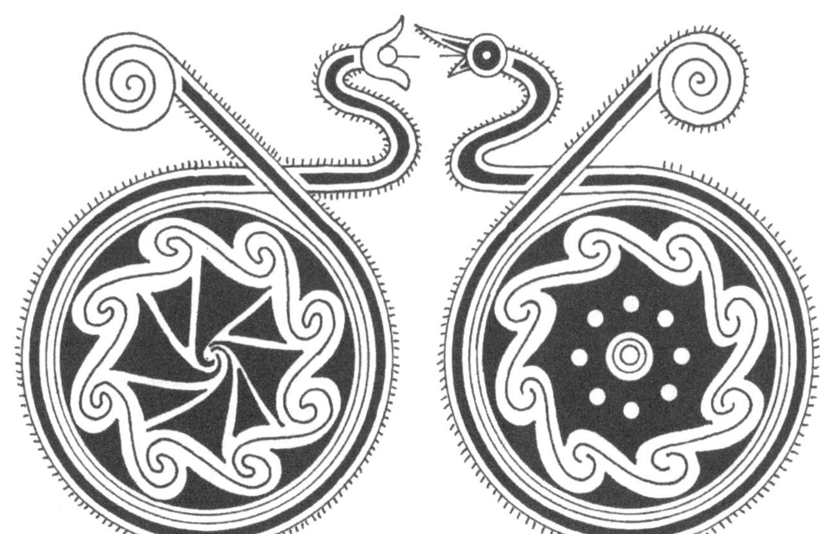

245 – Another motif from the above described stone. On the oldest series of picture Stones from Gotland one can see ornaments composed of rosettes – a bigger one in a form of swirling wheel above, and beneath it – a pair of rosettes similar to the one shown here. For other motifs from the same Stone, see No. 020, 187, and 244 [15.303-304, dwg. 11]

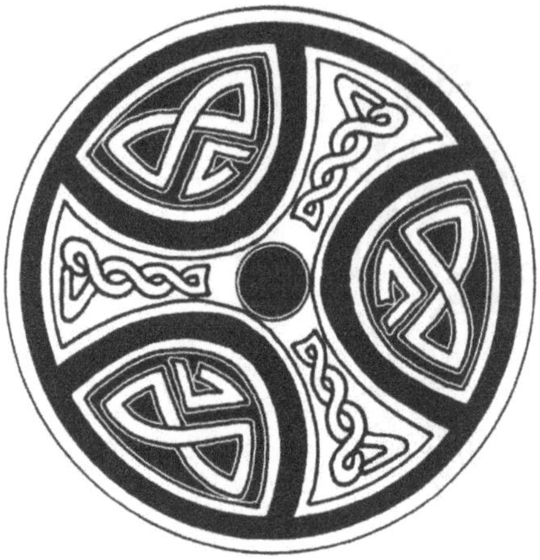

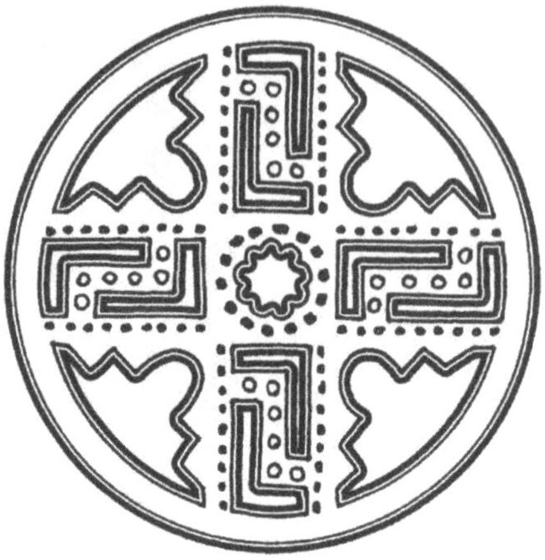

246 (left) – Upper part of a round fibula with plait patterns. Gotland, ca. 700-750 CE, [11.Table. 224, Fig. 1834; 10.65, Fig. 1834]

247 (right) – plate from the Frankish region (Also see No. 257) [3.203]

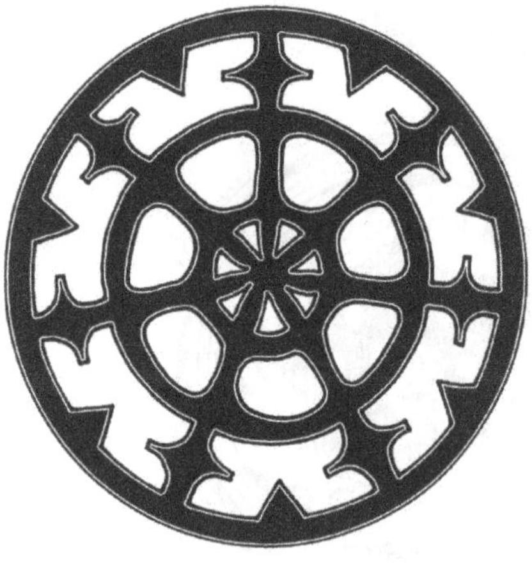

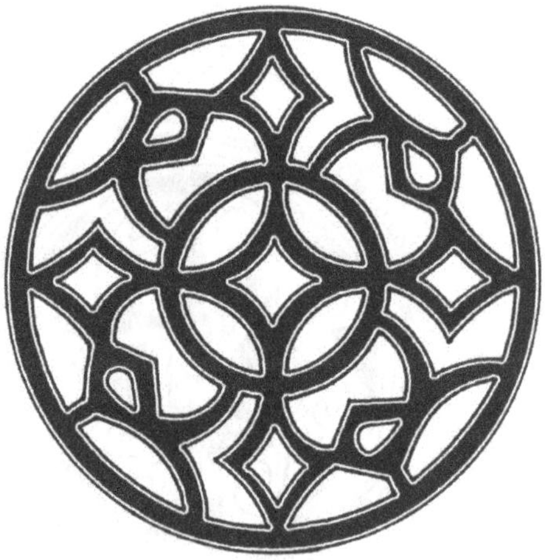

248 (left) – Cut-work panel with geometric ornaments. Gotland, ca. 700-750 CE [11. Table 228, Fig. 1882; 10.67, Fig. 1882]

249 (right) – Cut-work panel with four later Animal Style II figures cut out. Gotland, ca. 650-700 CE [11.Table 174, Fig. 1456; 10.54, Fig. 1456]

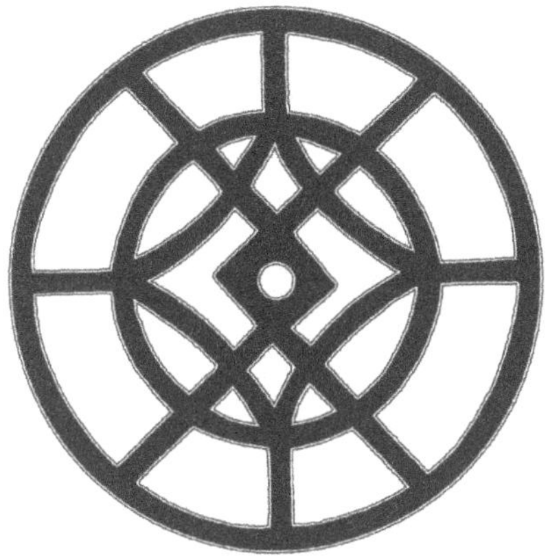

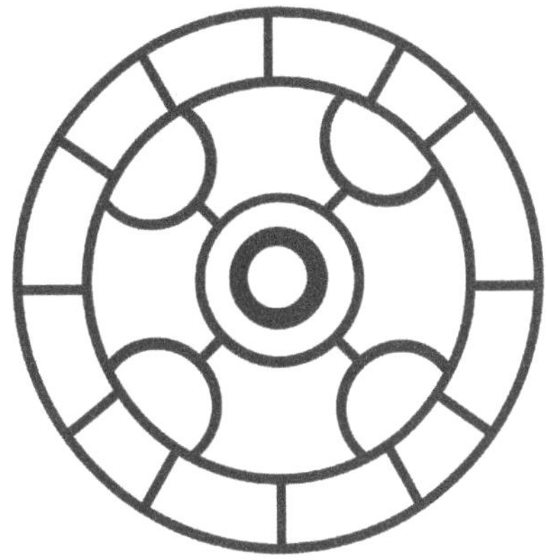

250 (left) – Cut-work panel with geometric ornaments. Gotland, ca. 600-650 CE [11. Table 113, Fig. 979; 10.40, Fig. 979]

251 (right) – Detail of the decorations on a sword pommel with Christian symbols. Dinham, Shropshire (England), second quarter of the 7th c. [17.31]

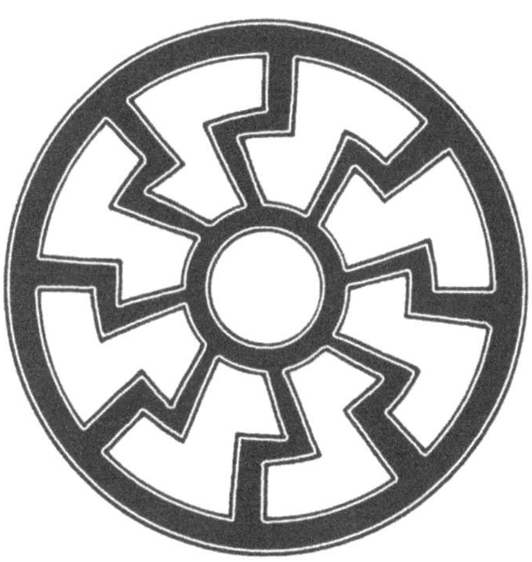

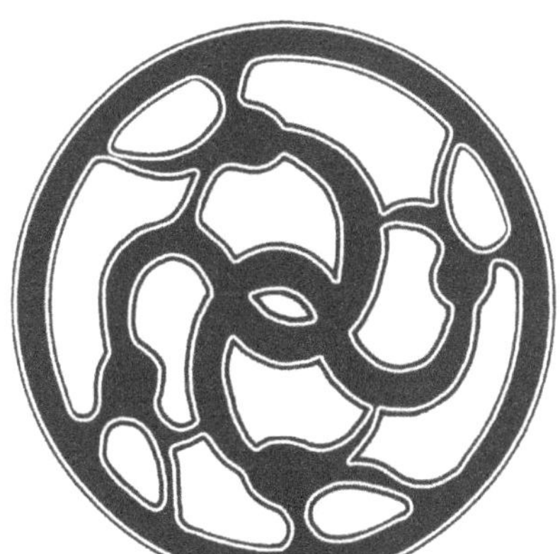

252 (left) – Bronze Alemannic panel representing the solar wheel. Karlich (Germany) [3. dwg. 63]

253 (right) – As above, with zoomorphic ornaments

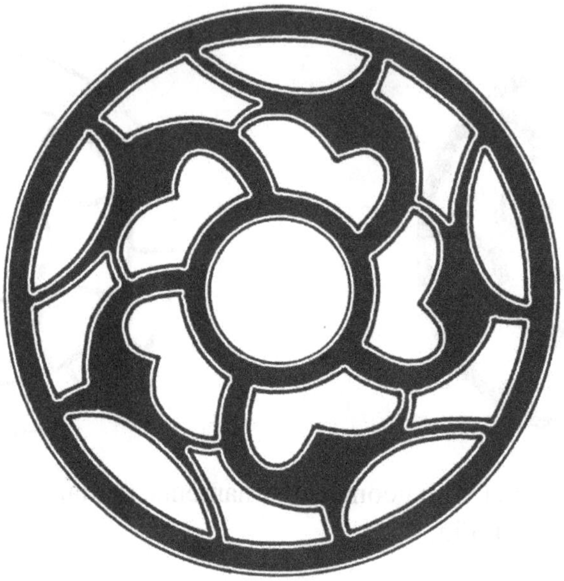

254 – Cut-work panel with five later Animal Style II figures cut out. Gotland, ca. 650-700 CE [11.Table 175, Fig. 1457; 10.54, Fig. 1457]

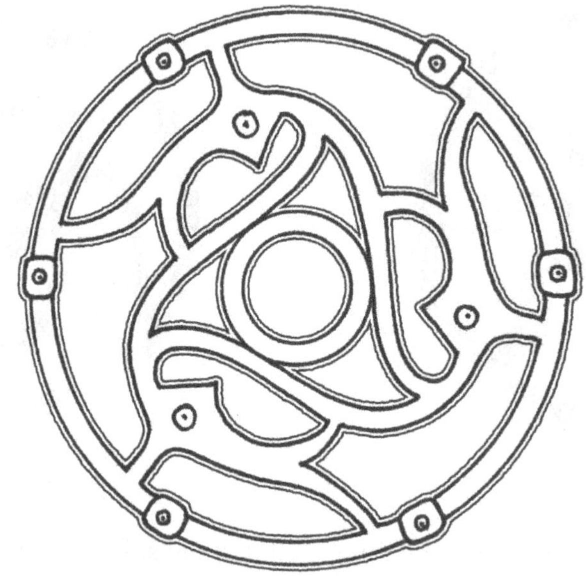

255 – Cut-work panel with three Animal Style II figures arranged into a triskelion. Gotland, ca. 600-650 CE [11.Table 113, Fig. 978; 10.39, Fig. 978]

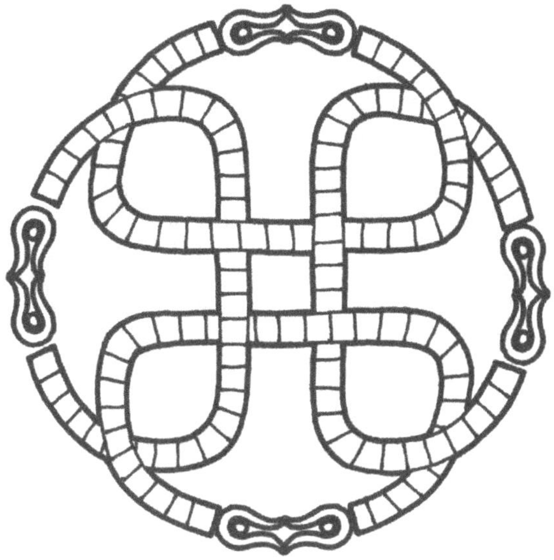

256 – Symbol arranged from serpents, the main ornament on a gold Alemannic brooch, with visible Lombardic influences. Wittislingen (Germany), 1st half of 7th c. (Also see 260) [3.103, dwg. 43]

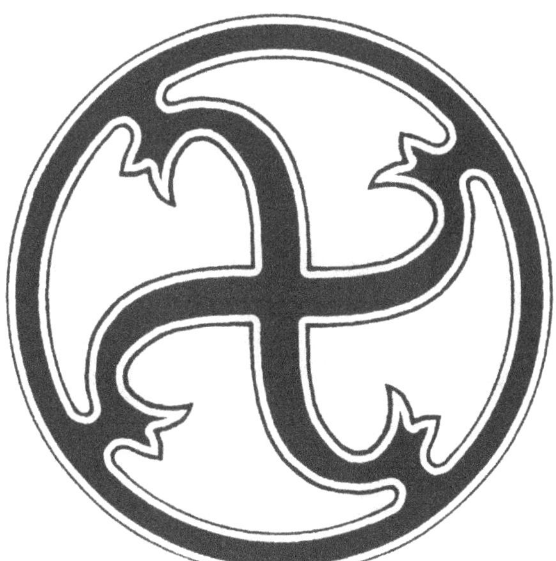

257 – See 247

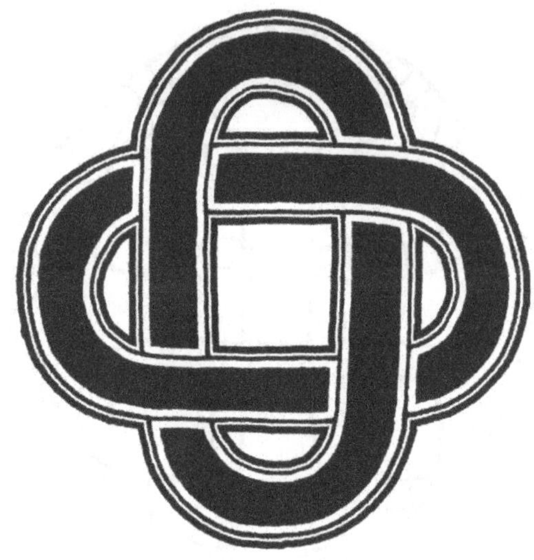

258 – See 154

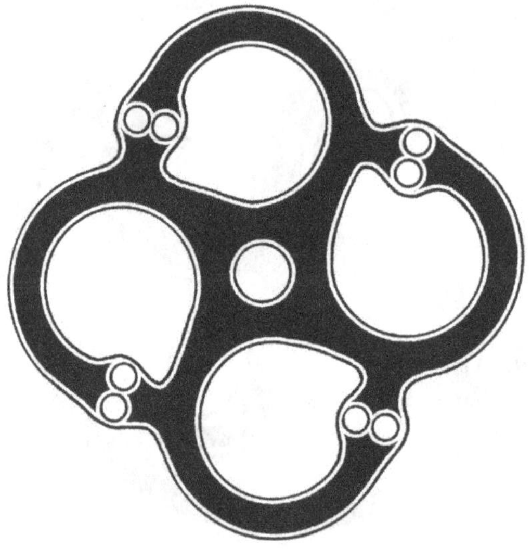

259 – Four serpents arranged in a swastika inside a cut-work fibula. Gotland, ca. 700-750 CE [11.Table 225, Fig. 1845; 10.66, Fig. 1845]

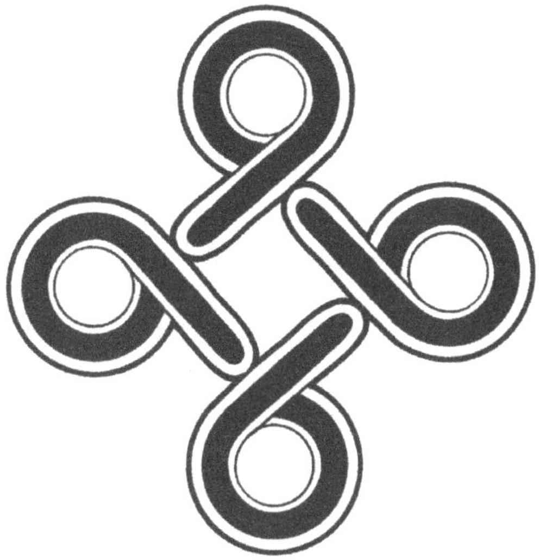

260 – Small ornament filling the empty space of the pattern from item 256) [3.103, dwg. 43]

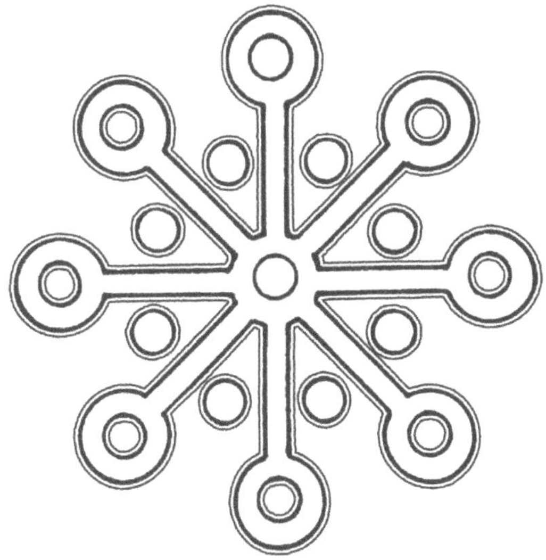

261 – Motif from a small plate on the tongue of an Ostrogoth belt buckle. Romagna (Italy), 6th c. (Also see 021) [12.61, Fig. 16]

SOURCES

1. Carver Martin, *Sutton Hoo, Burial Ground of Kings?,* London 2011.

2. Davidson Hilda Ellis, *The Sword in Anglo-Saxon England*, Woodbridge 1998.

3. Diesner Hans-Joachim, *Die Völkerwanderung*, Leipzig 1976;

4. Evans Angela Care, *The Sutton Hoo Ship Burial,* London 2010;

5. *Die Franken, Wegbereiter Europas. 5.-8.* Jahrhundert, Katalog Wystawy, Berlin 1997.

6. Jørgensen Erik, Petersen Peter Vang, *Nydam Bog – new finds and observations*, w: Jørgensen Lars, Strorgaard Birger, Thomsen Lone Gebauer, *The Spoils of Victory. The North in the shadow of the Roman Empire, Catalogue*, Copenhagen 2003; pp. 258-285.

7. Jørgensen Lars, Strorgaard Birger, Thomsen Lone Gebauer, *The Spoils of Victory. The North in the shadow of the Roman Empire, Catalogue*, Copenhagen 2003; pp. 365-435.

8. Leahy Kevin, *Anglo-Saxon Crafts*, Stroud 2012.

9. Mortimer Paul, *Woden's Warriors. Warffare, Beliefs, Arms and Armour in Northern Europe during the 6th and 7th Centuries*, 2011.

10. Nerman Birger, *Die Vendelzeit Gotlands im Auftrage der Kungl. Vitterhets Historie och Antikvitets Akademien,* Band I: 1.Text, Stockholm 1975.

11. Nerman Birger, *Die Vendelzeit Gotlands im Auftrage der Kungl. Vitterhets Historie och Antikvitets Akademien,* Band II. Taffeln, Stockholm 1969.

12. Palol de Pedro, Ripoll Gisela, *Die Goten. Geschichte und Kunst in Westeuropa,* Augsburg 1999.

13. Petersen Peter Vang, *Warrior art, religion and symbolism*, w: Jørgensen Lars, Strorgaard Birger, Thomsen Lone Gebauer, *The Spoils of Victory. The North in the shadow of the Roman Empire*, Catalogue, Copenhagen 2003; pp. 286-294.

14. Raynor Keith, *The Rempstone Mount*, East Lake 2010.

15. Rieck Flemming, *The ship from Nydam Bog*, Jørgensen Lars, Strorgaard Birger, Thomsen Lone Gebauer, *The Spoils of Victory. The North in the shadow of the Roman Empire*, Catalogue,

Copenhagen 2003; s. 296-309.

16. Szymański Wojciech, *Wokół skarbu z Martynowki*, w: "Kraje słowiańskie w wiekach średnich. Profanum i sacrum", Poznań 1998, pp. 357-365.

17. Webster Leslie, *Anglo-Saxon Art*, London 2012;

18. Williams Gareth, *Treasures from Sutton Hoo*, London 2011.

Look for these other books published in conjunction with Triglav

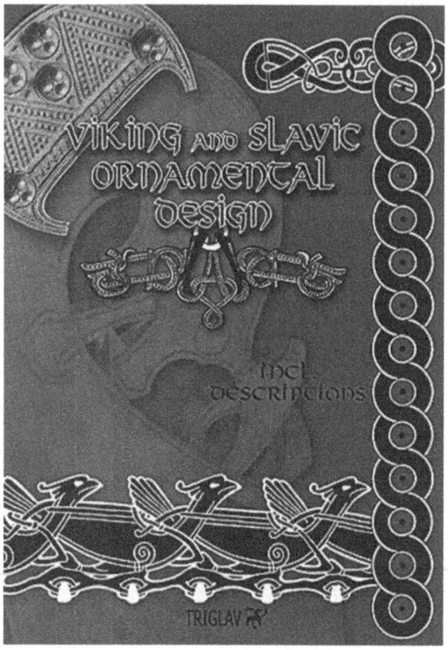

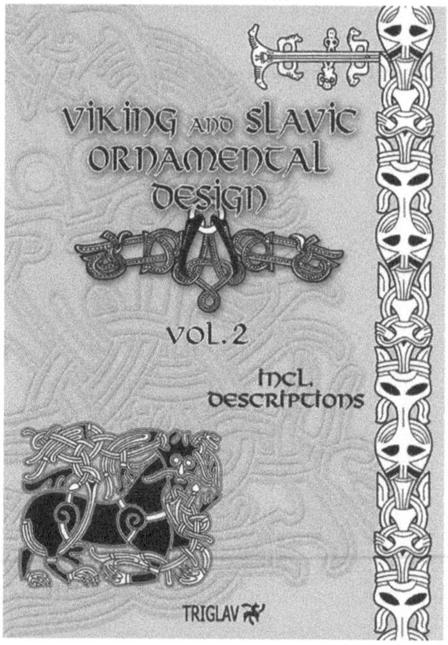

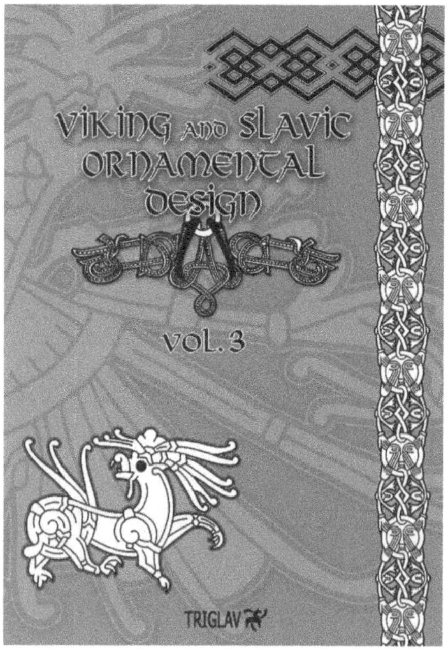

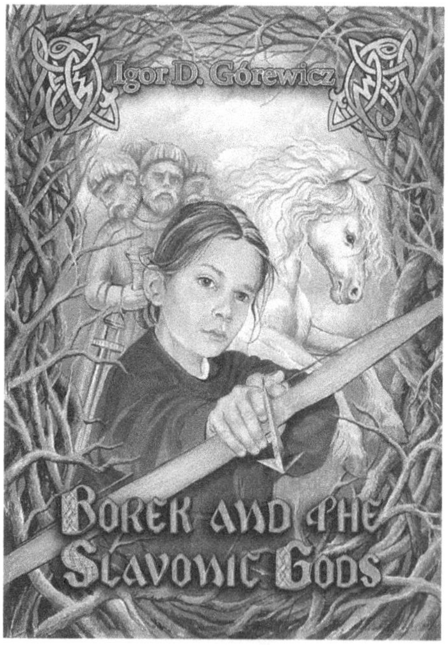

Look for more books from Winged Hussar Publishing, LLC – E-books, paperbacks and Limited-Edition hardcovers. The best in history, science fiction and fantasy at: https://www. wingedhussarpublishing.com or www.whpsupplyroom.com or follow us on Facebook at: Winged Hussar Publishing LLC Or on twitter at: WingHusPubLLC For information and upcoming publications

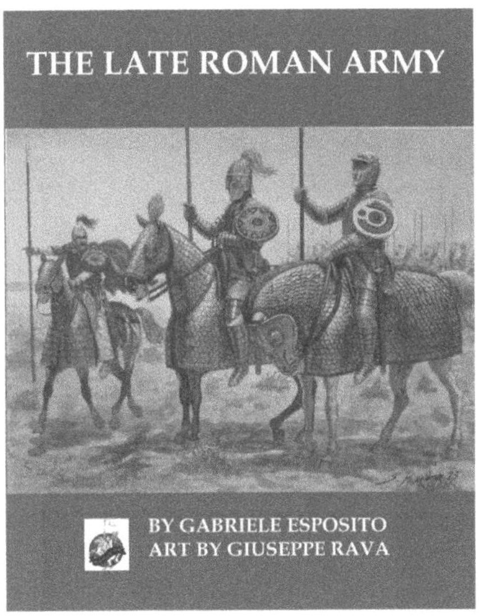

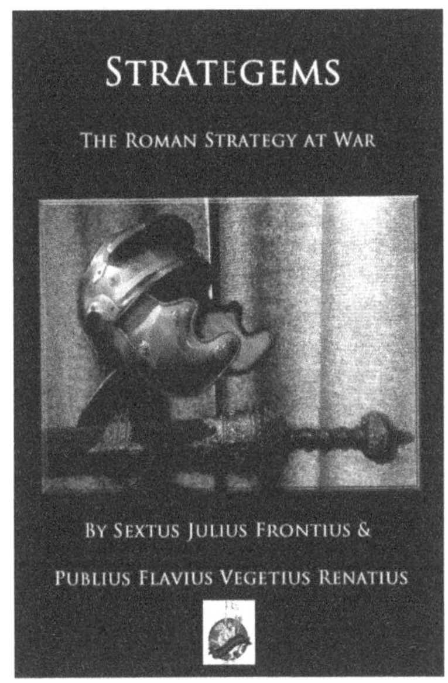

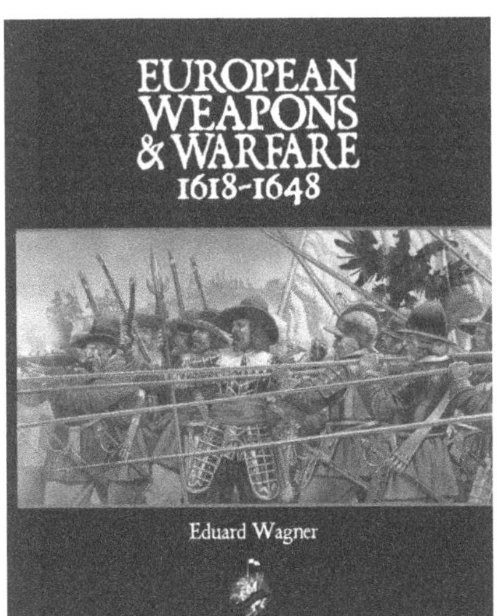

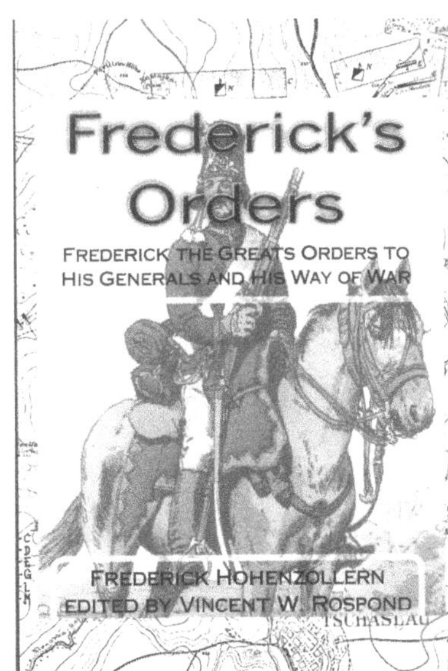